Acknowledgments

To my God and Father, whose grace abounds in my every endeavor, I am humbly grateful. Your guidance has been my source of refuge and solace, carrying me through this incredible journey.

To my beautiful family – Jaymie, Je`Chaun, Jenna, and Jaymie II – your unwavering love and support are the bedrock on which I stand. My heart overflows with gratitude for the joy and strength you bring to my life.

My dear siblings Tricia, Michael, Damian, Karim, France, and Chester, you are not just siblings but the fiercest of friends. Your encouragement and presence in my life are among my greatest blessings.

To my amazing aunts and uncles– Doreen, Grace, Eulin, Errol, Arnold Kelly, and Dorett Thompson – my love for you deepens with every moment. The wisdom and care you have showered upon me are treasures I hold close.

My heartfelt homage to Auntie Kaye (Marie Hodgson) and Auntie Lorna Williams. You have sown into my dreams with such generosity, and for this, I am eternally grateful. Your contributions have not only enriched this book but have shaped the very essence of who I am as a person.

Finally, a salute to the tireless Mr. Lawrance Martin, the administration, dedicated pastors, and my esteemed colleagues at the Allegheny East Conference. Alongside you in the field, amidst challenges we faced, our shared commitment has forged not just advancements for our organization but a camaraderie that I deeply value.

This book is a testament to all of you, and to the collective spirit of perseverance and heart that you represent. Thank you for being the pillars of inspiration and love in my life.

With Love – Chauna-Kaye

Contents

Chapter 1. The Case for Sound Risk Management...... 1

Chapter 2. Risk Management Theory for Church Officers... 11

Section I - Governance

Chapter 3. The Sacred Responsibility of Church Officers... 21

Chapter 4. Understanding Evolving Challenges in the Modern World 27

Chapter 5. Establishing a Governance Structure to Support Risk Management 29

Chapter 6. Risk Management Education and Awareness at Your Church 35

Chapter 7. Developing a Culture of Safety in Your Ministry 41

Section II - Protecting the People

Chapter 8. The Heart of the Matter—People Protection... 49

Chapter 9. Child Protection: Ensuring the Well-Being of the Most Vulnerable 51

Chapter 10. The Psychological, Emotional, and Spiritual Impact on Victims of Child Sexual Abuse 55

Chapter 11. Legal Exposure of Child Abuse 59

Chapter 12. Preventing Child Sexual Abuse at
Church.. 67

Chapter 13. Trust, Authority, and the Grooming
Process 87

Chapter 14. Confronting the Culture of Silence 93

Chapter 15. Personal Injury (Accident) Prevention 99

Chapter 16. Employment Practices 109

Chapter 17. Ministerial Exception 125

Chapter 18. Creating a Safe Environment through
Sound Ergonomic Practices............................ 131

Chapter 19. Rendering Unto Caesar: The Importance
of Legal Compliance.......................................137

Chapter 20. Insurance Coverages Required for
Employees 149

Chapter 21. Supplemental Insurance Coverages 153

Chapter 22. Volunteer Management 157

Section III - Protecting the Property

Chapter 23. Securing Sacred Spaces: Facilities
Management for Houses of Worship 163

Chapter 24. Managing Construction Projects in Faith
Communities 169

Chapter 25. Burglary and Theft Prevention 183

Chapter 26. Active Shooter Events: Preparation and
Response 193

Chapter 27. Cyber Risk Awareness and Prevention .. 199

Protecting the Sacred

A Church Officer's Guide to Effective Risk Management

Chauna-Kaye Pottinger

TRILOGY CHRISTIAN PUBLISHERS
Tustin, CA

TRILOGY

Trilogy Christian Publishers
A Wholly Owned Subsidiary of Trinity Broadcasting Network
2442 Michelle Drive
Tustin, CA 92780

Protecting the Sacred: A Church Officer's Guide to Effective Risk Management

Copyright © 2024 by Chauna-Kaye Pottinger

All Scripture quotations, unless otherwise indicated, are taken from the Holy Bible, New Living Translation, copyright © 1996, 2004, 2015 by Tyndale House Foundation. Used by permission of Tyndale House Publishers, Inc., Carol Stream, Illinois 60188. All rights reserved.

All rights reserved, including the right to reproduce this book or portions thereof in any form whatsoever.
For information, address Trilogy Christian Publishing
Rights Department, 2442 Michelle Driye, Tustin, CA 92780.
Trilogy Christian Publishing/ TBN and colophon are trademarks of Trinity Broadcasting Network.
For information about special discounts for bulk purchases, please contact Trilogy Christian Publishing.
Trilogy Disclaimer: The views and content expressed in this book are those of the author and may not necessarily reflect the views and doctrine of Trilogy Christian Publishing or the Trinity Broadcasting Network.

10 9 8 7 6 5 4 3 2 1

Library of Congress Cataloging-in-Publication Data is available.

ISBN 979-8-89333-275-9

ISBN 979-8-89333-276-6 (ebook)

Praise for *Protecting the Sacred: A Church Officer's Guide to Effective Risk Management*

"*Protecting the Sacred: A Church Officer's Guide to Effective Risk Management* addresses a critical need for churches to proactively manage the myriad risks that can impede their mission. With practical insights and actionable suggestions, this book illuminates key areas where church leaders should take caution."

- Jackson Doggette Esq.

"Impressive, extensive, effective and practical for pastors and ministry leaders, is how I characterize *Protecting the Sacred: A Church Officer's Guide to Effective Risk Management*. Chauna-Kaye Pottinger's critical insights and passion for safety and protection are clearly stated in every chapter. As a seasoned pastor and administrator who has served the church for 53 years, I take no reservations in recommending this important resource to pastors and other church leaders."

- D. Robert Kennedy, EdD; PhD - Senior Pastor

"*Protecting the Sacred: A Church Officer's Guide to Effective Risk Management* asserts that understanding the balance between ministry and safety is critical to the overall success of a church in an engaging and easy to read format. I appreciated the principles and credible safety structure set forth herein, as it will enable church leadership teams to think proactively about their risk management strategy."

– Heather Hilliard Esq.

Chapter 28. Protecting the Funds: Fraud Prevention at Church 209

Chapter 29. Should We Rent or Should We Buy? 217

Section IV - Protecting the Reputation of Your Ministry

Chapter 30. Managing the Reputation of Your Ministry 225

Chapter 31. Managing Crisis with Effective Communication 229

Chapter 32. Responding to Financial Scandals 237

Chapter 33. Managing Social Media and Online Presence 241

Chapter 34. Conflict Resolution within the Congregation 249

Chapter 35. Preserving the Reputation of Your Ministry after a Scandal 255

Chapter 36. Legal Issues Affecting the Reputation of Your Church 259

Conclusion 261

Appendix 1: Sample Action Investigation Form 263

Appendix 2: Sample Church Safety Officer Job Description 265

Appendix 3: Sample Church Safety Committee Charter 270

Appendix 4: Sample Child Protection Policy 274

Appendix 5: Cyber Risk Vulnerability Checklist 278

Notes 281

CHAPTER 1

The Case for Sound Risk Management

In the dimly lit corridors of St. Philip and St. James Episcopal Church in Denver, a story of betrayal and tragedy unfolded—a somber reminder of the imperative need for robust risk management practices within the sacred walls of our places of worship. Mary Tenantry-Moses was an unsuspecting soul seeking spiritual counselling from Father Paul Robinson, the assistant priest at the center of this heart-wrenching saga. Little did Mary know that her quest for spiritual guidance would plunge her into a nightmarish abyss of pain and regret. Father Robinson was aware of Mary's delicate mental health history, yet he callously pursued a forbidden relationship with her, unleashing a devastating cascade of consequences.

As the clandestine affair unraveled, Mary's mental fragility reached a breaking point, shattering the sanctity of her marriage, further plunging her into the relentless grip of psychiatric care. The court's subsequent ruling in favor of Mary exposed an even more disturbing saga, one that reeked of negligence on the part of the key decision-makers at the Episcopal Diocese of Colorado, an utter failure on their part to implement the safeguards entrusted to protect vulnerable members like Mary.

Armed with knowledge of Father Robinson's struggles, his battles with depression, self-esteem, and a muddled sexual identity, the Diocese neglected their duty to disclose this pertinent information to the team of leaders at the church when appointing him to a position of spiritual authority. The court echoed the gravity of their missteps, as it became evident that the church failed to recognize the warning signs of Father Robinson's inappropriate conduct, even when Mary's concerned brother-in-law, after learning the details of the affair, sounded the alarm.

The consequences of the Diocese's negligence were profound, etching a price tag of over **$1.2 million** in damages. Mary, once seeking spiritual guidance within the church's embrace, emerged from the ordeal with her mental health in tatters, and her family life completely destroyed.[1]

In the case of Moses v. Diocese of Colorado, we are exposed to a cautionary tale, beckoning us to recognize the all-encompassing impact that sound risk management practices can have in protecting our sacred institutions. It challenges us to take courageous steps to shield our communities, ensuring that they remain a safe space, untainted by the malevolent intentions of those who exploit positions of trust. In the echoes of this heartbreaking story is a clarion call to safeguard the spiritual havens that countless individuals innocently seek in times of vulnerability.

Churches are on a mission to transform lives through their community involvement, worship services, and fulfilling the spiritual needs of their members. Understanding this, the need to implement comprehensive protocols that will anticipate threats and proactively respond in a manner that will preserve and protect this mission becomes paramount. When ministry activities are pursued without these measures, it can precipitate significant financial ramifications, mar the esteemed reputation of the local church, and erode the trust vested by the community in the institution at large. Consequently, the adoption of proactive measures to prevent such occurrences and to diligently work toward cultivating safer and healthier communities is central to the operations of communities of faith.

If you should plug in the word "sacred" into any search engine, it would yield results like connected with God" or "dedicated to a religious purpose." The things that are considered to be sacred within any community of faith are valued as treasures that are to be protected and preserved. Leaders and other key decision-makers within our churches are the true heroes of our faith, entrusted with the solemn duty of safeguarding the three most sacred pillars that form the bedrock of religious entities: *people, property,* and *reputation*. As they step into the arena of responsibility, they must embrace their roles as guardians poised to defend against the unseen adversaries that threaten their congregations' very safety and security.

These valiant heroes of faith are not just strategizing for their community's spiritual growth but also for the physical well-being of all who will join their communities. So, what I need you to do is to personalize this mission. Because the hero I speak of is you. It is your reliance on God's wisdom and the sound risk management guidance you are exposed to in this book that will serve as your sword and shield against the unpredictable challenges that may arise.

In this book, we will discuss how your decisions can extend the church's mission beyond its traditional boundaries. Through the lens of sound risk management practices, your church may become the catalyst for growth, innovation, and resilience, propelling the church into uncharted territories with unwavering faith and strategic acumen.

Yet the stakes are even higher. The burden to ensure the protection of the most vulnerable members within your community also rests with you. This book unveils church leaders' profound responsibility as they navigate the intricate landscapes of risk to shield the most susceptible from harm and exploitation—children, seniors, and the disabled.

Broken down into four main sections, we first address the most fundamental element in the implementation of sound risk management practices—establishing a robust governance structure. The next three sections each focus on one of the three sacred elements within communities of faith. We first discuss the church's number one asset—its people. Then we provide insights and guidance on how you may protect the church's property. Finally, we address the role of risk management in preserving the reputation of your church.

The Biblical Case for Risk Management

Some church leaders are of the opinion that churches should prioritize ministry—discipleship, evangelism, and spiritual growth—over concerns about risk management. This stance often stems from a misunderstanding of how risk management underpins the church's mission. Risk management does not compete with ministry activities; effective risk management completes it. The Adventist Risk Management's slogan encapsulates this harmony perfectly: "Our ministry...is to protect your ministry." When done correctly, risk management not only safeguards ministry initiatives, it also enables leaders to honor their sacred duty of responsibly stewarding the lives entrusted to their care.

Scripture lends firm support to the concept of proactive caution. Proverbs 27:12 advises the wise to foresee danger and take measures to avoid it, emphasizing foresight and wisdom. Similarly, Galatians 6:2 calls on us to bear one another's burdens, reinforcing the importance of safety measures in safeguarding our congregations, particularly the most vulnerable members. Furthermore, the parable of the talents in Matthew 25:14-30 contrasts fear-based risk management with strategic, thoughtful risk-taking. Jesus praises those who judiciously manage risks to yield gains, teaching us that managing risks effectively involves measured consideration and action, not their complete elimination.

The Numbers Mean Something

For nine years I've immersed myself in the study of losses. Through this journey, I've come to realize how easy it is to become lost in the intricacies of a data-driven approach to risk management, losing sight of the deeper significance behind the numbers. While data offers valuable insights and provides a factual backdrop to our response strategy, there is a much more significant meaning beyond the numbers.

On January 17, 2016, I sat in our conference room with other church leaders, absorbing the shocking reality presented to us. The road ahead seemed daunting. For years, our group insurance accounts carried a loss ratio of a staggering 107 percent. Seventy-six percent of the losses paid were attributable to property claims. While our insurance carrier liked us as a client, I am sure they didn't like those numbers. My eyes drifted from the charts and tables to the description behind these large losses.

Water damage, personal injury, and child sexual abuse were just the tip of the iceberg. Beyond these numbers are many stories, stories like that of Deacon White, who sustained injuries while volunteering his time at the church. His injury threatened the very survival of his family, who relied exclusively on him as the primary provider.

Behind these numbers was the catastrophic damage done to buildings because of natural disasters, which also meant crippled ministry activity caused by the displacement of members, who because of unsafe conditions in their own worship facilities were forced to gather in other spaces.

Having reviewed the stories behind the numbers, it was made clear to me that we had to act, and this action needed to be swift and effective. It was then that an idea came to me - we needed to completely revamp our risk management program.

My first observation was that 85 percent of the losses experienced were preventable. Leading the list of major losses was water damage stemming from frozen pipes. Collaborating closely with our insurance carrier, we initiated a rigorous education and awareness campaign aimed at equipping our leaders with preventive measures against such losses. Subsequently, the installation of temperature and water sensors within our buildings proved to be a pivotal advancement that substantially reduced incidents.

By systematically analyzing both the quantitative and qualitative factors that contributed to our losses, we were able to not only bring our loss ratio down to a more manageable 24 percent, but we also improved the quality of our worship spaces, built a more risk-aware culture, and ultimately created a safer environment for our employees, volunteers, and members.

Risk Management: a Righteous Imperative

The call to ministry is a noble endeavor marked by devotion to the spiritual well-being of congregants and the spreading of the gospel to surrounding communities and, by extension, the world. Yet amid the pursuit of living the gospel, the journey has its share of uncertainties and potential pitfalls. Slips, trips and falls, child sexual abuse, lawsuits, dilapidated facilities, and fraud are all challenges places of worship must contend with daily.

Navigating the intricate landscape of risks within ministry demands a concerted team effort led by key members of church leadership. A dedicated commitment to safeguarding the sacred foundations of any ministry—its people, property, and reputation—is paramount. Unattended vulnerabilities in any of these three pillars directly threaten our ministry's sustained operation. To ensure the enduring vitality of a ministry, intentional and proactive measures must be taken to address and mitigate potential threats to these fundamental elements.

Protecting the Sacred: A Church Officer's Guide to Effective Risk Management is a comprehensive exploration into the indispensable realm of risk management within the context of church ministry. Drawing from the timeless wisdom of Scripture, the collective experiences of seasoned spiritual leaders, and the invaluable insights of risk management professionals, this work seeks to illuminate the importance of anticipating, understanding, and effectively mitigating the diverse risks that ministers, church officers, and congregations may encounter.

We will delve into the intricacies of risk assessment, crisis preparedness, and ethical considerations while recognizing that a well-managed ministry is spiritually robust and resilient in the face of challenges. As stewards of our faith, we are responsible for ensuring that the paths we tread are illuminated not only by the light of divine purpose but also by the discernment and foresight required to safeguard the spiritual integrity of our communities.

This book is not a mere guide but a call to action. It beckons ministers, pastoral teams, and congregational leaders to embrace a proactive stance in addressing the multifaceted risks that can impact the sacred mission of their faith community. Through practical strategies, real-life case studies, and a rich reservoir of theological reflections, we will equip the servants of God with the tools necessary to navigate the complexities of the modern ministry landscape.

Once again, thank you for joining me on this transformative expedition into the heart of ministry risk management. Together, let us cultivate a culture of preparedness, wisdom, and resilience, ensuring that our sacred endeavors endure and thrive, fortified by a steadfast commitment to the spiritual and material well-being of those we are called to lead.

CHAPTER 2

Risk Management Theory for Church Officers

If you already have a deep understanding of the risk management process, you may want to skip this chapter and move on to chapter 3. If not, consider this chapter to be a crash course in risk management theory. We will explore the risk management process comprising risk identification, risk assessment, risk response (prevent, accept, avoid, and transfer), and risk monitoring and controlling, and provide practical examples for church officers to apply these concepts in their leadership roles.

Risk Identification

Risk identification involves recognizing potential threats and opportunities that may impact the church's objectives. Church officers should engage in a systematic process of identifying risks across various aspects, such as financial, operational, reputational, and hazard.

Financial Risks: Church officers should assess the risk of financial instability due to unforeseen circumstances, such as economic downturns or unexpected expenses.

Operational Risks: Identify risks related to day-to-day activities, like disruptions to regular services due to technical failures or logistical issues.

Reputational Risks: Consider potential damage to the church's reputation, such as public controversies or negative media attention.

Hazard Risks: Hazard risk at a church refers to the potential dangers or threats that could adversely affect the safety, well-being, and operations of the church community. These hazards may encompass a wide range of events, including natural disasters (such as earthquakes, floods, or storms), fire hazards, security concerns, and health emergencies. Recognizing and addressing hazard risks is vital for the church leadership to implement proactive measures that ensure the safety of congregants, protect church assets, and maintain the continuity of essential activities in the face of unforeseen events.

Risk Assessment

Once risks are identified, the next step is to assess their likelihood of occurrence and potential impact. Church officers can use a risk matrix to evaluate the factors that threaten their operations. The risk matrix is a vital tool that can provide an organized and visual method for evaluating the risks that a ministry organization faces. By placing potential hazards on a grid based on the severity of their impact and the likelihood of their occurrence, church leaders can prioritize risks, which allows them to focus resources and attention on the most significant threats. This approach helps to ensure not only the safety and well-being of the congregation and church property but also the continuity of church activities. The simplicity of the risk matrix enables it to be easily understood by all members of the church's risk management team, fostering clear communication and effective decision-making.

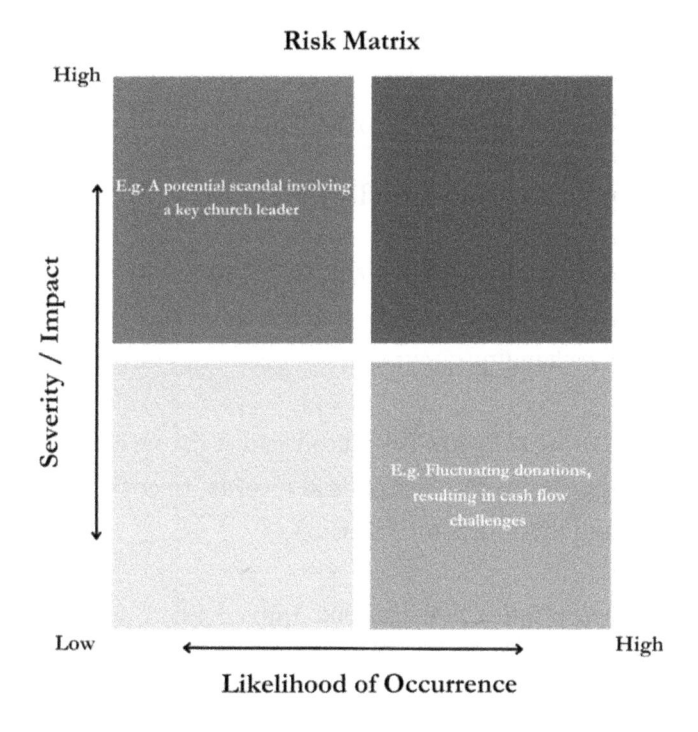

Risk Matrix

A chart with "Severity / Impact" on the vertical axis (Low to High) and "Likelihood of Occurrence" on the horizontal axis (Low to High). The upper-left quadrant contains: "E.g. A potential scandal involving a key church leader". The lower-right quadrant contains: "E.g. Fluctuating donations, resulting in cash flow challenges".

Risk Response

After assessing risks, church officers must develop strategies for response. This involves deciding whether to prevent, accept, avoid, or transfer the risk.

Prevent: Implement internal controls and policies to prevent financial mismanagement or potential conflicts of interest.

Accept: Recognize that certain risks, like changes in attendance due to external factors, are inherent to the church environment and may need to be accepted.

Avoid: If a particular initiative carries substantial legal or reputational risks, consider avoiding it altogether.

Transfer: Purchase insurance to transfer financial risks, such as property damage or liability claims.

Risk Monitoring and Controlling

Once risk responses are in place, continuous monitoring is essential to ensure effectiveness of the response chosen and to adapt to changing circumstances. Examples include:

Regular Financial Audits: Periodically enlist the service of external agencies to review financial records, to ensure compliance and identify potential issues.

Ongoing Reputation Management: Implement a system to monitor public perception (e.g., Google reviews and social media commentary) and address potential reputational risks promptly.

The Difference Between Risk Tolerance and Risk Appetite

The safest church in the world is a closed church. The challenge with a closed church is that there is no ministry activity taking place; people's lives are not being positively impacted through a well-knit community of faith; worship activities are not conducted; and community outreach activities are not happening. I always say we do not want to practice risk *elimination*; we practice risk *management*. This is why it is important for churches to determine their risk tolerance and risk appetite. In the context of church and ministry, risk tolerance and risk appetite differ primarily in their approach to managing uncertainties and challenges.

Risk Tolerance

Risk tolerance refers to the level of uncertainty or adversity that a church or ministry is willing to accept or withstand before taking action. In this context, risk tolerance often reflects the organization's ability to endure potential negative outcomes or setbacks while remaining committed to its mission and values. Churches and ministries with a low risk tolerance may prioritize caution and conservative decision-making, opting for strategies that minimize the likelihood of failure or controversy. Factors influencing risk tolerance in this context may include the organization's financial stability, reputation, and commitment to adhering to ethical or doctrinal principles.

Risk Appetite

Risk appetite describes the willingness of a church or ministry to actively seek out and embrace opportunities, even if they involve a degree of uncertainty or potential risk. In contrast to risk tolerance, risk appetite reflects an organization's eagerness to innovate, grow, and expand its impact, sometimes by venturing into uncharted territory or challenging existing norms. Churches and ministries with a high-risk appetite may be more inclined to pursue ambitious initiatives, engage in outreach efforts to new demographics, or experiment with unconventional approaches to ministry. Factors shaping risk appetite in this context may include the organization's vision for growth, leadership philosophy, and willingness to adapt to changing societal or cultural dynamics.[1]

Overall, while risk tolerance emphasizes resilience and preparedness in the face of adversity, risk appetite underscores a proactive and forward-thinking approach to embracing opportunities for growth and impact within the context of church and ministry operations. Both concepts are essential for effectively managing uncertainties and maximizing the organization's potential to fulfill its mission.

Churches, like many secular organizations, stand to benefit immensely from a more holistic approach to risk management. Traditional risk management was more focused on a reactive approach to risks, only responding after an incident would have occurred, while a new concept called Enterprise Risk Management (ERM) takes a more proactive approach. This shift represents a recognition of the interconnected nature of risks and the need for a strategic, integrated approach to managing them within the context of the church's mission and goals.

The approach taken in this body of work is one that embraces ERM as a key strategy in combatting the multiplicity of challenges faced by faith-based organizations. If implemented as stated, your church will see a number of benefits, to include:

1. Heightened risk awareness at your church, which will inevitably lead to better decision-making as the church becomes more familiar with their own risk profile.
2. Enhanced resilience in the face of challenges will also be achieved. By proactively addressing risks and building resilience, churches can better navigate challenges and disruptions, thereby safeguarding their mission and continuity.
3. Improved confidence among key stakeholders is also achieved when robust risk management strategies are implemented. Donors, members and regulatory agencies love organizations that demonstrate in their practice that they are trustworthy.
4. Strategic alignment is much easier to achieve when risk management is integrated in the overall strate-

gic planning process, where the leadership applies foresight in embedding risk considerations in the pursuit of the church's mission and objectives.

By integrating risk management principles into their decision-making processes, church officers can better navigate uncertainties and protect the well-being of their congregation. The proactive identification, assessment, response, and monitoring of risks contribute to the overall resilience and sustainability of the church, enabling leaders to fulfill their spiritual mission while minimizing potential pitfalls.

Section I: Governance

CHAPTER 3

The Sacred Responsibility of Church Officers

Whether church officers are selected or elected, they are entrusted with a sacred responsibility that extends far beyond the pulpit and board meetings. They are key decision makers who must work closely with senior leadership to identify, analyze, and respond to potential risks affecting the congregation. This shared burden demands a deep devotion to the three sacred pillars of ministry mentioned earlier—people, property, and reputation.

To be truly effective, church leaders must take a prayerful and proactive approach to risk management. This includes developing comprehensive policies and procedures, establishing clear communication channels and response protocols, and investing in the necessary training and resources to address emerging threats.

Make no mistake, the church officer's role in risk management is critical to the overall success of any ministry. From managing finances to ensuring safe physical spaces and promoting healthy relationships, their leadership is essential to creating a supportive and secure environment for the congregation. Only by valuing and prioritizing risk management can churches fulfill their mission and remain a trusted pillar of their community. It is through their discernment and strategic oversight that potential vulnerabilities are identified, addressed, and mitigated, fostering an environment of resilience and continuity.

Simultaneously, those charged with the day-to-day implementation of policies (office workers, ministry leaders, facilities managers, and other volunteers) shoulder a weighty responsibility in translating overarching strategies into tangible actions. These individuals are on the front lines of risk management execution. Their compliance with established policies, coupled with an acute awareness of the unique challenges faced by their ministry, contributes significantly to the overall effectiveness of risk management initiatives.

The Voice and Vote in Board Governance

"All in favor say aye!" Have you considered the weight of responsibility that rests with the response that goes with that question?

The power vested in the voice and vote of board members is not just a procedural formality; it is a potent force that shapes the destiny of your ministry. This authority becomes particularly significant when addressing matters that can impact the safety and security of church activities, such as the supervision provided during church trips. The duty of care for the congregation, especially for children and other vulnerable groups demands meticulous consideration. Leaders must not only be present in body but also in mind, contemplating the potential risks and measures needed to safeguard the flock entrusted to their care.

As a member of your church board or leadership team, it is imperative that you realize that a board vote takes on a profound meaning. It is not merely a show of hands; it is a pledge to uphold the biblical values and principles that the church stands for. Therefore, leaders must approach their role with a discerning mindset, asking probing questions that delve into the heart of the issues at hand.

Financial stewardship is another critical aspect of church governance that cannot be overlooked. Board members must thoroughly scrutinize financial reports to ensure transparency and accountability. Evidence of wrongdoing should be treated with the seriousness it demands. The fiduciary responsibility that comes with a board-appointed role requires leaders to be vigilant, guarding the financial integrity of the ministry, by not sacrificing the success of the ministry on the altar of personal and political expediency. By meticulously examining financial records, board members can unveil potential risks and prevent the church from falling prey to mismanagement or malfeasance.

The Four Behaviors of a Responsible Board Member

The manifestations of a successful and effective board will be evident in the embodiment of four primary behaviors by its members:

1. **Confidentiality:** Confidentiality is paramount when handling sensitive information discussed within board meetings. Members must respect the privacy of individuals involved in church matters, including staff, congregation members, and donors. Avoid discussing confidential matters outside of the boardroom, and refrain from sharing privileged information even within your personal circles. Upholding confidentiality fosters trust within the board and demonstrates integrity to the broader community.
2. **Conflict of Interest:** Recognizing and managing conflicts of interest is crucial for maintaining the board's integrity and impartiality. If you have a personal or financial interest that could potentially influence your decision-making, it's essential to disclose it transparently to the board. Knowing when to recuse yourself from voting on a particular issue is a mark of ethical conduct. Prioritize the best interests of the church above personal gain or affiliations and be willing to step aside from discussions or decisions where a conflict arises.
3. **Impeccable Record Keeping:** Accurate and thorough record-keeping is essential for accountability and transparency within the board's activities. Maintain detailed minutes of board meetings, including voted actions, decisions, and action items but never the discussions. According to Attorney Jackson Doggette, in case of a lawsuit, the intricate discussions that led

to a decision should not be part of the record as this can cause significant challenges during the discovery process. Keep records of financial transactions, budgets, and policies adopted by the board. These records not only serve as a historical reference but also provide documentation for audits, legal compliance, and continuity in leadership transitions. Embrace technology tools and systems to streamline record-keeping processes and ensure accessibility to relevant stakeholders.

4. **Active Engagement:** Active engagement entails more than simply attending meetings; it involves proactive participation in board discussions, decision-making, and initiatives. Prepare thoroughly for meetings by reviewing agendas, reports, and relevant documents in advance. Contribute constructively to discussions by offering insights, asking questions, and challenging assumptions when necessary. Take on leadership roles in board committees or special projects to leverage your skills and expertise for the benefit of the church's mission. Additionally, stay informed about current issues, trends, and best practices in church governance to continuously enhance your effectiveness as a board member.

CHAPTER 4

Understanding the Evolving Challenges in the Modern World

Today, the challenges facing churches and communities of faith have evolved in unprecedented ways. The dynamics of our contemporary landscape introduce a myriad of complexities that demand a nuanced and intentional response from those entrusted with the sacred mission of ministry. As the boundaries between the sacred and the secular blur, the need for robust risk management practices within the hallowed halls of faith becomes more imperative.

Legally, the landscape is fraught with intricacies that can ensnare the unprepared. From compliance with evolving regulations to navigating potential legal pitfalls, the modern church operates within a legal framework that requires much vigilance. Failure to address these legal dimensions can lead to consequences that jeopardize the institution's mission and place its very existence in jeopardy.

Operationally, the challenges are equally profound. The intricate dance between financial stewardship, logistical efficiency, and the management of human resources demands a delicate balance. In the absence of meticulous risk management practices, the operational heartbeat of a church risks disruption, impacting its ability to fulfill its spiritual calling and maintain the trust of its congregation.

Spiritually, the challenges are twofold. While the spiritual mission remains paramount, there also needs to be a practical dimension of risk management to ensure the ability to fulfill that mission. The sacred call to shepherd a congregation is inseparable from the responsibility to protect and sustain the environment in which that calling thrives.

Reputation, a currency of immeasurable value in faith-based communities, is equally at stake. In an era of instantaneous communication and heightened public scrutiny, the repercussions of reputational damage can be swift and severe. Ignoring sound risk management practices puts at risk not only the image of the church but also the trust and credibility built over years of faithful service.

The journey ahead is one of empowerment, equipping church officers to embrace their pivotal roles as intentional stewards of risk. Through a blend of strategic insights, real-world case studies, and hands-on tools, this book aims to transform risk management from a daunting obligation into a proactive and empowering aspect of leadership within ministry. My intention is to inspire church officers to lead with confidence, foresight, and a steadfast commitment to the sacred mission they have been called to serve.

CHAPTER 5

Establishing a Governance Structure to Support Risk Management

Implementing a sound risk management program within faith-based organizations requires the establishment of a governance framework to support the successful implementation of policies and procedures. This is one of the most crucial steps that leaders must take to achieve a high standard of effective risk management. Governance in risk management involves a number of factors, but for the purpose of this book I will stick to the following important elements:

1. Appointing a church safety officer
2. Establishing a safety, or risk management, committee
3. Developing risk management policies and protocols
4. Adopting a risk assessment tool to manage top risks
5. Establishing a risk management training program

By establishing a governance structure, communities of faith will not only recognize the diverse risks they face but also proactively engage in intentional strategies that fortify their resilience. In this next section, we advocate for the establishment of a comprehensive governance framework underpinned by key pillars that collectively contribute to the seamless integration of risk management within the fabric of any ministry.

Appointing a Church Safety Officer

The number one step in establishing a governance structure is to appoint a church safety officer. This dedicated individual serves as a point guard, spearheading risk management initiatives with a specialized focus on safety and security. Their responsibilities encompass risk assessment, policy enforcement, and the cultivation of a safety-conscious culture. By appointing a church safety officer, faith communities demonstrate a commitment to prioritizing the well-being of their congregants, staff, and assets.

In the Appendix of this book, a copy of a safety officer job description is provided and will also be made available on the Protecting the Sacred website as a free resource for your ministry. Feel free to download a copy and adapt it to the unique needs of your ministry. This Safety Officer Job Description is available in English, French, Spanish, and Korean.

Establishing a Safety, or Risk Management, Committee

Beyond individual roles, the establishment of a safety, or risk management, committee further solidifies the governance framework. This committee serves as a collaborative hub where diverse perspectives converge to identify, assess, and address potential risks.

Through the words of Solomon in Proverbs 11:14, we see the best support for this concept. "Where no wise guidance is, the people fail; but in the multitude of counselors, there is safety." Through regular meetings and strategic deliberations, the committee becomes a proactive force, ensuring that the ministry remains agile and responsive to evolving challenges.

Earlier we promised that we would provide practical guides along with tools and resources to help in the establishment of sound risk management planning within your ministry organization. In addition to the Safety Officer Job Description, we also provide a Safety Committee Job Description in the Appendix. Feel free to also download a copy from the Protecting the Sacred website.

It is important to note that there are circumstances in which it becomes impossible to establish a safety committee, based on the size of the congregation. In these cases, we strongly recommend that the governing board functions as the church safety committee and that specific time be designated on the agenda of their meetings for safety matters to be addressed by that body.

Drafting Policies and Protocols

The drafting of comprehensive policies and protocols is also a critical component within this governance structure. Addressing a spectrum of risks, from child protection, accident prevention, fire drills, and business continuity planning to financial risks, these policies form the bedrock of a resilient ministry. By articulating clear expectations and procedural guidelines, faith communities lay the groundwork for a systematic and standardized approach to risk management.

Compliance with Established Policy

As a seasoned risk management expert experienced in dealing with numerous cases involving churches, I cannot stress enough the importance of adhering to policies that are put in place. In my line of work, one of the recurring themes I have encountered from attorneys is that it is far better to have no policy than to have one that is not adhered to.

Policies are a vital aspect of managing ministry risks. They provide a framework for how activities should be conducted which could ultimately minimize the impact of negative risks. However, drafting a policy alone is not enough. Ensuring compliance with these policies is just as crucial.

Non-compliance with policies is a major source of risk for churches. It can leave the church exposed to liability and other legal challenges that could be detrimental to its operations. Therefore, it is of utmost importance that policies are adhered to and reviewed regularly to ensure they remain relevant and effective.

Furthermore, churches should consider having a system in place for monitoring compliance. This could be in the form of regular internal audits, training sessions for staff and volunteers, or clearly defined reporting mechanisms for incidents that violate established policies.

Developing Risk Assessment Tools

The efficacy of risk management hinges on the ability to identify and prioritize potential threats. To this end, developing risk assessment tools tailored to the unique context of a faith community is essential. These tools serve as diagnostic instruments, enabling leaders to pinpoint key areas of risk exposure so that the allocation of resources can be strategically implemented as part of the mitigation of vulnerabilities.

There are many tools that can be used for this purpose. For example, the Risk Register is a popular tool used within many secular organizations and on projects to evaluate top threats. This one tool helps the leadership team to go through the entire risk management process during a brainstorming session.

There are other less complicated risk assessment tools, such as safety checklists for drivers, church self-inspection surveys, and child abuse vulnerability checklists. A self-inspection survey is a very effective resource for churches in the identification of vulnerabilities in a church's overall risk management program.

Safety officers use this tool once per year to assess the building and other aspects of the risk management process. The result of the assessment is then used to inform the projects that they will take on for the year. The church self-inspection, along with other tools, are included in the tools and resource section of the Protecting the Sacred website.

CHAPTER 6

Risk Management Education and Awareness at Your Church

Integral to this governance structure is the establishment of a well-rounded safety training program. This initiative ensures that newly elected officers and employees are equipped with the knowledge and skills necessary to navigate potential risks. Through targeted training sessions, faith communities not only foster a culture of awareness but also empower their leaders to respond effectively in crisis situations.

I have tested and proven this to be true. It is essential for leaders at every level of the church to be aware of safety best practices and understand how to implement them in their respective ministries. Youth leaders, Sabbath/Sunday School teachers, choir directors, deacons, and elders, all have a role to play. Their actions at the departmental and individual level help in shaping a church culture that prioritizes safety, which can significantly aid in the successful implementation of sound safety management programs ministry wide.

A culture of safety in the church is built on education and awareness. Church leaders must understand that safety is not just the absence of incidents; rather, it involves a set of best practices that must be followed to prevent hazardous incidents from occurring. When church leaders are continually educated and aware of these best practices, they can be part of creating a safe environment for everyone in the church. This can be achieved in several ways:

1. Provide on-demand online courses.
2. Enlist the services of a risk management expert.
3. Host onsite training of key volunteers and church officers.
4. Establish a day of safety emphasis.

Provide On-demand Online Courses.

To aid in the education of church leaders on safety best practices, there are several tools and systems that can be employed. One such tools is on-demand online courses. Online courses provide church leaders with an opportunity to learn at their own pace and convenience. For example, Ministry Safe has a very robust set of online courses for the training of youth leaders and educators in child protection.

These courses offer a very easy and convenient option for staff and volunteers, and are usually designed to be interactive and engaging, enabling church leaders to learn and understand safety practices at a deep level. Doing this also can be very helpful in providing a trail of due diligence to demonstrate that your organization is committed to safety by offering documented proof that church officers have completed the training and have demonstrated mastery of the materials by completing assessments.

Enlist the Service of Risk Management Experts.

Additionally, churches can invite risk management experts to lead training sessions. These experts are usually equipped with extensive knowledge and experience in identifying and managing risks in various environments. They can provide valuable insights on safety, best practices, and precautionary measures. This kind of training not only educates church leaders but also provides them with an opportunity to ask questions and clarify any doubts they may have.

Host Onsite Training for Key Volunteers and Church Officers.

As you seek to build a risk-aware culture, one of the most effective ways to do this is to dedicate one or two days out of the year specifically for onsite training sessions for church officers. You can either bring in outside experts as mentioned above or have qualified in-house members lead sessions on various topics that are essential to your ministry operations. For example, one of our churches hosted first aid and CPR training sessions for their youth leaders. Another one of our churches hosted training sessions for youth leaders and other essential volunteers on how to detect abuse of minors.

This can be a fun way to build bonds outside of routine worship sessions. Make it fun by having the session catered and incorporate activities or scenarios that will keep the participants engaged.

Establish a Day of Safety Emphasis.

While we usually focus on spiritual and religious aspects of worship, embracing a day of safety reminds us of the importance of physical safety and security within our church community.

This day of safety can be used as an opportunity to educate and raise awareness among the members. Church leaders can take the time during the service to emphasize different aspects of safety, such as conducting a fire drill or showing a video about or raising awareness of safety.

Fire drills are essential in any organization, and churches are no exception. Conducting fire drills regularly ensures that everyone is aware of exit routes and knows what to do in case of a fire. It also provides an opportunity to identify and rectify any potential fire hazards.

Showing videos about safety can be an impactful way to raise awareness within the church community. Numerous safety-related topics can be covered, like driving safety or home security. Raising awareness about child abduction and human trafficking is also critical, because these are rampant problems in our society.

In addition to these events, the church can also invite external organizations or speakers to educate the community about safety issues. This can be helpful in learning about new safety practices and laws and how to keep the church safe in our ever-evolving world.

Embracing a day of safety promotes a culture of safety within the church community. It shows that the church leadership takes safety and security seriously and is proactive in creating a comfortable and safe environment for everyone. It also reinforces the message that the well-being of each member is essential to the church as a whole.

The tools and systems available to educate church leaders include online courses, inviting risk management experts to lead in training, hosting onsite training sessions, and establishing a day of safety. When these best practices are put in place, the church becomes a safe and secure environment for everyone.

CHAPTER 7

Developing a Culture of Safety in Your Ministry

The culture of your church and ministry will go a very long way in securing the success of your risk management and safety efforts. This doesn't just end with establishing policies and procedures; it also models the behaviors and practices that you want to see replicated in the areas of safety compliance.

Embracing the Notion of Best Practice.

To effectively manage risks in a church setting, it is essential to embrace the notion of best practice. This involves conducting extensive research into the most successful safety practices for the specific risks you are responding to, determining the effectiveness of such a response, and adapting it to suit the needs of your ministry. Drawing upon the principles of benchmarking can greatly enhance the effectiveness of your safety measures and enable you to make informed decisions that uphold the safety of your congregation.

One concrete example of best practice in safety is the installation of security cameras. These devices provide an excellent means of monitoring activities both inside and outside the church building, which can help identify suspicious activities that pose a potential threat to the safety and security of the congregation. By increasing the level of situational awareness, this simple yet effective measure can go a long way in ensuring the safety of your church.

Another crucial area for embracing best practice in safety is by developing comprehensive emergency preparedness plans. These plans should outline the necessary steps to be taken in the event of various emergencies, such as fires, medical crises, or security breaches. A well-designed emergency plan provides clear guidance, assigns specific responsibilities, and ensures that everyone in the church is well-informed and equipped to respond appropriately to an emergency.

Embracing the concept of best practice in safety and risk management is a critical step in fostering a culture of safety. By benchmarking successful safety practices, such as security cameras and emergency preparedness plans, churches can significantly improve their safety measures and protect the well-being of their congregations.

The Importance of Role Modeling

Of all the factors that help in carving out a culture of safety, role modeling is probably the most important. When the behaviors and practices that you want to see imitated are visible to other members of the faith community, it increases the likelihood of compliance.

Church leaders should lead by example, adhering to established safety policies and procedures. This can be done by wearing appropriate safety gear when required, following established safety protocols, and attending safety training sessions.

Over-Communicating the Importance of Safety Compliance

As a leader, you have a great responsibility in communicating the need for compliance with safety protocols and guidelines. It is your duty to ensure that every member of your organization understands the importance of safety and is willing to follow the necessary procedures to keep everyone safe.

One of the most effective ways to influence the behaviors of your members is through repetition. By repeatedly highlighting the importance of safety compliance, you can unlock the power of your words and shape the culture of safety in your organization.

As John Maxwell says, "a leader is one who knows the way, goes the way, and shows the way."[1] It is up to you to lead by example and communicate the need for safety compliance to your members. By doing so, you can inspire them to become safety advocates themselves.

To achieve this goal, it is important to use all available communication channels to promote safety compliance. This may include highlighting certain rules and guidelines in your church's announcements, bulletins, and pastoral remarks.

Another practical step you can take is to reward members who demonstrate a commitment to safety compliance. By doing so, you can incentivize members to follow safety protocols and help create a culture of safety in your organization.

Through the power of your words and effective communication, you can influence the behaviors of your members and create a culture of safety in your organization. Remember, safety is not just about rules and guidelines, it is about people—and people matter.

Adopt Safety as a Core Value within your Organization.

The success of any ministry organization rests on more than just its ability to provide vibrant and stimulating worship services to members and service attendees. It also hinges on the values and norms that underpin the culture of that community of faith. I strongly recommend that churches adopt safety as one of their core values. This one step can go a long way in shaping the overall culture of safety, while equally enhancing the effectiveness and longevity of the organization.

Core values are vital to an organization's strategic direction, as they include the beliefs, attitudes, behaviors, and practices that guide decision-making, employee conduct, and customer experience. Therefore, building a culture of safety means that safety must be a fundamental principle within the organization.

In the past, pastors and members have seen churches and ministries as havens for spiritual growth and development. However, recent events, including shootings, fires, and acts of terrorism, have highlighted the need for a culture of safety within these sacred spaces. Strong core values can help to ensure that the necessary safety measures are put in place to safeguard people within the organization.

Embracing safety as a core value requires intentional action from the leadership, staff, congregation, and ministry partners. Clear communication of the new core value is vital and must be achieved through training, awareness campaigns, and continuous reminders. Leaders must ensure that safety assessments are conducted, emergency protocols are established, and safety committees are established to oversee the implementation of safety measures.

The adoption of safety as a core value has several benefits for churches and ministries. These benefits are not limited to the church or ministry but also extend to its members, partners, and the community.

Section II: Protecting the People

CHAPTER 8

The Heart of the Matter—People Protection

This next section focuses on the safeguarding of our most treasured assets - the lives of those who gather to worship and find community within our churches. We will shed light on the often-overlooked aspects of congregational safety and preparedness.

The sanctity of our churches is not determined solely by the strength of our spiritual guidance but also by the robustness of our protective measures. We are bringing to you an exploration of topics that sit at the heart of our collective responsibility. Through the coming chapters, we will traverse the dimensions of child protection, personal injury prevention, the nuances of employment practices, guidelines for trips and activity safety, and procuring the right insurance coverage – all with the intention of cultivating a secure sanctuary for our faith to flourish.

Our purpose transcends the mere listing of safety protocols; we invoke a paradigm shift in the perception of church leaders. This section is for every church leader who recognizes that the decisions made can—and should—reflect the value we place on human life.

CHAPTER 9

Child Protection: Ensuring Well-Being of the Most Vulnerable

The subject matter of child protection is so extensive and impactful that it merits its own dedicated discourse. Its significance extends well beyond ministry activities, casting a profound shadow on the lives of the vulnerable victims ensnared when institutions fail to implement adequate precautionary measures.

Let's take a moment to do some roleplaying. I want you to envision yourself as a caring and assertive shepherd entrusted with safeguarding a flock. I am sure that you would likely be committed to the task of erecting fences or barriers to shield these precious, vulnerable sheep from any and all threats.

But what happens in the hypothetical scenario when you discover that within those protective confines lies a cunning wolf disguised as a sheep, patiently awaiting the right moment to go on the prowl? I am sure that the most pressing questions on your mind would be, "How do we respond to this insidious threat? How do we peel the curtains back and unveil this wolf in sheep's clothing?" I assure you that the worst possible response is complacency. This concealed wolf would wreak havoc on the unwitting sheep if your vigilance as a shepherd wavers.

Expert after expert has asserted that there are no known profiles of a typical child sexual abuse perpetrator. Perpetrators of this awful act are men, women, teens, and children from every nationality and race. Gone are the days when we could use measures like separating children based on their genders, because the risk of same-sex, child-on-child abuse is emerging as a threat as well. We must remain vigilant when entrusted with the sacred duty of supervising children.

In commenting on the safeguards we must erect to protect the innocent lives entrusted in our care, Gregory Love, co-founder of Ministry Safe,[1] highlighted that we need a paradigm shift in our approach—a shift from building pitiful picket fences to the construction of fortified fortresses. The metaphorical fortresses we build are not just symbolic; they are integral within the context of child protection. In the sections that follow we will delve into the intricacies of safeguarding the most vulnerable members within our communities —our children.

We are often overtaken by a misguided notion that the threats to child safety within our communities of faith are external, but this could not be further from the truth. Yes, external threats do exist, but the greatest threat we face as a church is posed by the wolf in sheep's clothing who engages in behaviors that on the surface appear innocent, while they are actively planning or inflicting harm on the ones most vulnerable within our communities. This is a fact that is supported by research. Most child abuse cases are inflicted by people these children know and trust.

Children, disabled members, and the elderly are among the most vulnerable members of any faith community. I believe wholeheartedly that the true metal of a faith-based organization is put to the test when we see how they treat the most vulnerable among them. Let's do everything within our power to protect them. The strategies outlined in this book are helpful to protect all vulnerable groups within our faith communities. We will first assess the spiritual, psychological, and emotional impact of the abuse, after which, we will examine the step we can take to build fortresses.

CHAPTER 10

The Psychological, Emotional, and Spiritual Impact on Victims of Child Sexual Abuse

Countless words have been dedicated to exploring the tangible aftermath of child sexual abuse. It's widely acknowledged that such experiences hinder a child's journey towards becoming a flourishing adult. However, amidst these discussions, have we truly delved into the intricate realms of psychological and spiritual repercussions? The scars left by childhood sexual abuse run deep, infiltrating the very core of their entire being. The breach of trust, especially when perpetrated by figures within religious communities, engenders a tumultuous landscape of guilt, shame, and enduring emotional trauma. This chapter explores the profound depths of these wounds, illuminating the unseen impacts that shape the lives of survivors.

Sexual abuse is a heinous crime that can leave lasting emotional, psychological, and spiritual scars on victims. While the physical and emotional effects of such abuse are more widely recognized, there is often little focus on the profound spiritual impact it has on survivors. Sexual abuse can raise some of the most fundamental spiritual questions for survivors, leaving them grappling with issues surrounding their faith, religious institutions, and even the concept of a higher power.[i]

For many, organized religion plays a significant role in their lives and forms a part of their identity. It provides a sense of community, purpose, and comfort. However, the abuse of trust by individuals who should epitomize the safety and comfort of a faith community can cause a profound rupture in one's connection with God.

The survivors' encounter with betrayal often reverberates through the fundamental aspects of their spiritual equilibrium. In certain cases, it gives rise to an overwhelming cognitive dissonance, prompting a profound reevaluation of their convictions and instigating a crisis of faith. The sacred refuge intended for guidance, healing, and solace may tragically metamorphose into a venue marred by anguish, apprehension, and the profound sting of betrayal.

Furthermore, such experiences can lead to a sense of helplessness and hopelessness that can negatively affect the survivor's mental health, leading them to suffer long-term depression, anxiety, and even post-traumatic stress disorder. They may struggle with trust issues, struggle to form close relationships, and struggle to heal from the psychological trauma.

The violation of trust through such abhorrent acts can lead to a significant rupture in one's connection with God, and the aftermath can cause a personal and spiritual crisis that is often ignored. It's imperative to provide support and resources for survivors, as they navigate the painful journey of healing and try to find a sense of peace, comfort, and spirituality.

The spiritual journey of survivors is marked by the echoes of their traumatic experiences. Questions of worthiness, divine purpose, and the very nature of a benevolent higher power may become shrouded in doubt. The sacred space that should foster spiritual growth and understanding becomes tainted, leaving survivors to grapple with a distorted perception of their place in the divine mission and calling upon their lives.

Moreover, the spiritual impact extends beyond the individual, rippling through the broader faith community. The revelation of child sexual abuse fractures the collective trust and challenges the core tenets of compassion and protection that should define a spiritual family. The erosion of faith in the institution can lead to a collective crisis, testing the resilience of the community's shared beliefs.

To address the spiritual impact of child sexual abuse is to acknowledge the nuanced intersection of trauma and faith. Healing must extend beyond physical and psychological realms to encompass the restoration of spiritual well-being.

Faith communities must stand as beacons of support and empathy, recognizing the delicate journey survivors undertake to reclaim their spiritual identities.

CHAPTER 11

Legal Exposure of Child Abuse

From a legal standpoint, there are primarily four main ways in which a church is viewed by the courts or a jury as negligent in relation to child protection. If an incident should occur at your church, the way the courts weigh a decision between negligence and gross negligence is highly dependent on the degree of perceived due diligence exercised in preventing and/or responding to an incident of child sexual abuse. A church can be found negligent in four main areas:

1. Negligent selection (hiring)
2. Negligent retention
3. Negligent supervision
4. Neglect of fiduciary duty

Negligent Selection (Hiring)

Negligent hiring in the context of child protection involves the failure to thoroughly screen and assess individuals who will be working with and in contact with children at the church. It is very easy to overlook this as an important measure, considering that many churches have difficulties finding volunteers to serve; as such, they strive to make the selection process as easy and seamless as possible. So instead of carrying out the required due diligence to properly screen volunteers, we cut corners.

Negligent Retention

Negligent retention involves keeping individuals in positions that allow for contact with children despite knowledge or suspicion of inappropriate behavior. Even with the best screening measures in place, some employees with predatory behavior may still slip through the cracks. As such, when an allegation is brought to the attention of ministry leaders, or church officers, it is imperative that all allegations are taken seriously and investigated.

One of the best practices to implement is that whenever someone has been accused of sexual abuse or misconduct, they should be immediately removed from their role while an investigation is conducted. If this allegation involves minors, the local investigating authorities with direct responsibilities over these matters are to be contacted.

While the authorities investigate, the church should also conduct its own investigation, as there are certain behaviors that are inappropriate but not criminal, and if the behavior breaches the code of conduct outlined by the church, then disciplinary action should be taken in compliance with the established code of conduct.

Negligent retention happens when a church:

1. Fails to act on reports or complaints of inappropriate conduct involving children.
2. Allows staff or volunteers with a history of misconduct to remain in child-related roles.
3. Ignores warning signs or red flags of potential harm to children.

Some of the main steps that may be taken to avoid these risks are by:

1. Establishing a robust reporting system for concerns related to child safety.
2. Implementing a thorough investigation process for reports of misconduct.
3. Having clear policies and procedures for the removal of individuals from child-related roles pending investigations.
4. Placing anyone accused of inappropriate behavior on administrative leave or removing them from their role to protect both them and the alleged victim.

Negligent Supervision in Child Protection

Negligent supervision transpires when oversight and control over activities involving children fall short of the required standard. Its manifestations are varied, each representing a potential breach in the protective fabric we strive to weave for our young and vulnerable congregants.

One glaring sign of negligent supervision surfaces when there is an insufficient number of supervisors for church events or activities involving children. This deficiency in personnel undermines the comprehensive vigilance required to ensure the safety and well-being of our youngest community members. The table below provides guidance on the most appropriate adult-to-child ratio to maintain for planned activities within our churches. [iii]

Ages	Adult:Child Ratio
Infants: Younger than 12 months old	1 adult should care for no more than 3 infants
Toddlers: 13–35 months old	1 adult should care for no more than 4 toddlers
Preschoolers: 3 years old	1 adult should care for no more than 7 preschoolers
Preschoolers: 4 years old	1 adult should care for no more than 8 preschoolers
Preschoolers: 5 years old	1 adult should care for no more than 8 preschoolers
School-age children: 6–8 years old	1 adult should care for no more than 10 school-age children
School-age children: 9–12 years old	1 adult should care for no more than 12 school-age children[ii]

Equally problematic is the failure to enforce safety protocols and guidelines, a lapse that could, in many instances, cause accidents and unforeseen incidents. The commitment to child safety extends beyond rhetoric; it hinges on the meticulous implementation of established measures designed to shield our children from harm. Neglecting this responsibility poses a direct threat to the sanctity of our protective efforts.

A further dimension of negligent supervision materializes when appointed supervisors neglect to exercise the necessary level of due diligence. This oversight can pave the way for situations where harm befalls our children, jeopardizing the very essence of our commitment to their security and well-being.

In understanding the gravity of negligent supervision, it is crucial to recognize its real-world implications. At a church lock-in, a 10-year-old was lured to an isolated section of the building and sexually assaulted by a 16-year-old, who noticed that all adult chaperones were busy preparing snacks for the children, leaving them unsupervised.

This example underscores the urgency with which we must address and rectify instances of negligent supervision within our faith communities. It is not merely a procedural flaw; it is a compromise of the sacred trust we bear to protect the most vulnerable among us. Proper supervision of those left within our care is a cornerstone in the edifice of a safe and nurturing environment for all.

Sometimes we spend much time and effort trying to identify adult predators, when in fact, we also need to be on the lookout for child predators as well. Child-on-child incidents have been known to be one of the primary ways in which abuse has taken place, whenever there are gaps in the level of supervision we provide.

Neglect of Fiduciary Duty

One of the most distressing forms of exploitation for a child is child sexual abuse, especially in church where children are supposed to be in a safe and protective environment. In such instances, it is crucial for the responsible parties, including the church leaders and staff, to uphold their fiduciary duty towards the children under their care. Neglecting this duty can lead to devastating consequences, both for the victim and the integrity of the institution.

Neglect of fiduciary duty involves the failure to act with a high level of care, trust, and responsibility to protect another individual, especially when they are vulnerable. Neglect of fiduciary duty is a severe breach of trust, particularly in instances of child sexual abuse in church. In the case of a survivor of child sexual abuse, the church leaders and staff have a fiduciary duty to ensure that children are protected from harm, regardless of the circumstances. The church should take all possible measures to prevent abuse from happening, including implementing background checks on all employees who interact with children, establishing strict policies and protocols for reporting suspected abuse cases, and ensuring that all reports of abuse are promptly investigated.

If a church fails to uphold its fiduciary duty and neglects child sexual abuse, it can result in lifelong trauma for the victims, leading to emotional distress, behavioral problems, and long-term physical health complications. Furthermore, it can also cause significant reputational damage to the institution, resulting in a loss of trust within the community and legal repercussions.

Those in positions of authority and responsibility have a significant obligation to protect vulnerable members of society and should take proactive steps to prevent such abuse from happening. By upholding their fiduciary duty, they can help minimize the risk of abuse and create a safe and secure environment for all members of the community.

CHAPTER 12

Preventing Child Sexual Abuse

Ensuring the safety and well-being of all congregants, especially the vulnerable children who seek solace within these walls, is an unequivocal priority. To fortify these sanctuaries against the harrowing specter of child sexual abuse, meticulous measures must be implemented. The first line of defense involves the careful selection of volunteers, with a stringent application process and comprehensive background screening.

Furthermore, the implementation of the "six-month rule," which will be discussed in more detail later in this chapter, stands as a critical safeguard, allowing sufficient time to assess the character and commitment of potential volunteers. The emphasis on supervision is indispensable, as seen through the enforcement of the "two-adult rule," the application of an open-door policy, and the proactive prevention of child-on-child abuse. A robust child safety policy serves as the backbone, underpinning the institution's commitment to safeguarding its youngest members.

The implementation of a code of conduct for volunteers ensures clear expectations and ethical standards, fostering an environment where the well-being of every child is paramount. These multifaceted measures collectively weave a protective shield, reinforcing the commitment of the church to create a secure haven for all who seek spiritual refuge within its embrace.

Conducting Background Screening

In some jurisdictions, conducting background screenings for anyone working with children is required by law, giving very little room for this decision to be left up to the entity. In other cases, background checks are a requirement from insurance carriers as a condition of coverage. Regardless of who requires it, performing background checks on official volunteers and employees who will work directly with children is a best practice that should be implemented. Here is a list of appropriate background checks:

1. Criminal background checks
2. Child abuse registry checks
3. Employment/volunteer history verification
4. Personal and institutional reference checks
5. Social media screening

Criminal Background Checks

The purpose of the criminal background check is to identify any criminal history that may pose a risk to the congregation or is disqualifying for working with children. This screening takes a comprehensive review of local, state, and federal criminal records.

Unfortunately, many of the available screening mechanisms do not allow for international background checks, so for members joining congregations from overseas, their criminal history will likely not be captured in this aspect of the screening process. In these cases, the leaders may have to rely on institutional reference checks as the most important screening measure. Here are a few ideas on what to look for when reviewing the results of background screening information:

1. Identify convictions related to violence, abuse, or offenses against vulnerable populations.
2. Ensure compliance with relevant laws governing background checks.

Confidentiality of Background Check Information

One cannot overemphasize the importance of maintaining strict confidentiality surrounding background check information. This facet of volunteer management is not just a matter of ethics and respect for privacy but is deeply embedded in legal considerations that govern the screening processes.

Background checks are important, but confidentiality is equally important to the integrity of the volunteer screening process. In the United States of America, legal frameworks, such as the Family Educational Rights and Privacy Act (FERPA) and the Health Insurance Portability and Accountability Act (HIPAA), set forth stringent guidelines on the privacy of personal information, extending their protective reach to volunteers involved in child-centric activities.

Failure to uphold confidentiality can have severe legal implications for organizations entrusted with the care of children. Volunteer background checks often reveal sensitive information, including criminal records, financial history, and personal references. The inadvertent disclosure of such information not only violates the privacy rights of volunteers but can also expose organizations to legal actions, ranging from civil suits to regulatory sanctions.

One of the key principles guiding best practices in this domain is restricting access to background check findings to only those individuals who have a legitimate need for such information. This principle aligns with the concept of the "need-to-know" basis, ensuring that only authorized personnel with a direct responsibility for volunteer placement or supervision are privy to the results.

It is imperative to designate specific individuals or roles within the organization who have the authority to review background check findings. Typically, this responsibility falls within the purview of human resources, volunteer coordinators, or designated child protection officers. These individuals undergo specialized training to handle confidential information responsibly and are bound by strict codes of conduct.

Additionally, religious organizational leaders must establish robust internal protocols to govern the storage, transmission, and disposal of background check information. Digital databases should be encrypted, and physical records should be securely stored. Access logs should be maintained to track who has viewed or obtained such information, creating an audit trail that can be invaluable in demonstrating compliance with privacy regulations.

Child Abuse Registry Checks

To specifically address the safety of children in the church's care, where a person may have been engaged specifically in child abuse investigations for which no criminal charges may have been filed, it is highly suggested that this screening takes place to identify those who may have engaged in past behaviors that disqualify them from ever working with children. This database includes checks for individuals listed for child abuse or neglect. Your reason for conducting this screening includes:

1. Identifying individuals with a history of child abuse allegations, even if they were not charged criminally, to determine if the investigation proved the allegations to be substantiated or unsubstantiated.

2. Ensuring compliance with state and federal child protection laws. There are many states that require this screening as part of the selection process. It is very important that you familiarize yourself with the laws specific to the state in which you conduct ministry.

Following is a list of disqualifying behaviors that church leaders are to consider when selecting volunteers to work with children. If the volunteer has any of these listed on their record, they should not be selected for the role.

Disqualifying Behaviors of Children/Youth Volunteers

1. Sexual assault of a child
2. Physical abuse of a child
3. Causing mental harm to a child
4. Sexual exploitation of a child
5. Incest
6. Use of a computer to facilitate sex crime
7. Soliciting a child for prostitution
8. Sexual intercourse with a child age sixteen or older
9. Exposure
10. Possession of child pornography
11. Child sex offender working with children
12. Registered sex offender photographing children
13. Child neglect; abduction
14. Contributing to truancy
15. Hazing
16. Child unattended in vehicle
17. Leaving loaded firearm accessible to a minor
18. Receiving stolen property from a child

19. Tattooing a child
20. Battery
21. Battery of a witness
22. Battery or threat to a judge
23. Battery to an unborn child

Employment/Volunteering History Verification

When appointing volunteers to work with children, churches are responsible for conducting thorough due diligence to ensure that the chosen volunteers have prior experience and qualifications that are pertinent to their designated roles. This is especially critical when selecting youth pastors or leaders, given the nature of their responsibilities. To facilitate this process, the ministry leader or pastor typically performs a rigorous verification of the volunteer's or employee's employment history and relevant qualifications.

During this verification process, it's important to go beyond simply contacting the volunteers' previous employers or churches served. Additional methods, such as conducting an internet search, can be employed to validate the accuracy of the volunteers' resumés.

Additionally, the verification process should involve a comprehensive check of the volunteer's pertinent qualifications, ensuring that they possess the necessary skills and expertise to work effectively with children. For instance, if the volunteer claims to have previously worked with children, the verifier should ask detailed questions about their previous experience, level of involvement, and discern possible behaviors or red flags in their history that may disqualify them from the role.

By following these steps, churches can be confident in their selection of qualified volunteers and can ensure the safety and well-being of the children in their care. The verification of employment and qualifications is a crucial component of the process of finding the appropriate volunteers to work in the church's children's ministry.

Reference Checks

When screening individuals who express an interest in working with children, employment verification is undoubtedly a powerful tool for verifying a potential hire's work history. However, this is only one aspect of due diligence, and it is equally important to obtain a deeper understanding of an individual's character and work ethic. Engage in a comprehensive screening process by contacting personal and professional references provided by the individual in question.

When contacting references, keep in mind that institutional reference checks carry more weight compared to personal references. It is far better to do an internet search to find the contact information for the institution listed on the resumé. This way, you can be assured that the place you are calling is a valid organization and not just any number listed by the applicant.

While performing your reference check, you should ask questions that can elicit meaningful and insightful feedback, such as the individual's reliability, integrity, and interpersonal skills. This gives you a more holistic picture of the person in question, allowing you to make an informed hiring decision.

Additionally, the reference check phase helps to identify potential concerns or red flags raised by references. It is important to carefully consider any such concerns and not ignore them. The screening process is designed to protect the well-being of children, and thorough reference checks are an essential component in ensuring safety.

Ultimately, by demonstrating a commitment to due diligence, the church sends a message to its community, and to anyone involved, that the safety and security of children is their top priority.

Social Media Screening

In today's age of technology and social media, there is a lot we can learn about a person's thoughts and behavior from what they post online. Understanding an individual's online presence and behavior is a very crucial step in the screening process prior to selecting an employee. It involves conducting a review of publicly available social media profiles, carefully seeking out language, behavior, and activities that may disqualify or qualify them for the role they will take on as an employee or volunteer.

As part of this screening process, you will seek to do the following:

1. Identify any content inconsistent with the values of the church.

2. Respect privacy and avoid discrimination based on personal beliefs and preferences.

The Six-month Rule

As we navigate the intricacies surrounding child protection within faith communities, one way in which a church may effectively screen candidates working with children is through the process of observation. It is an imperative temporal dimension, a concept often encapsulated in what is colloquially known as the "six-month rule." This rule serves as a vital component of a comprehensive risk management strategy, offering a nuanced approach to the integration of new members who express an eagerness to engage with children within the faith community.

Picture this temporal threshold as a probation period, a safeguarding interval during which the community assesses the commitment and intentions of new members. This precautionary measure ensures a thoughtful and deliberate onboarding process, recognizing that trust is earned through time-tested dedication.

The rationale behind the six-month rule is multifaceted. First, it allows for a thorough vetting process, enabling the community to glean insights into the character and reliability of those who seek to play a role in the lives of children. During this period, leaders and fellow members can observe and evaluate the newcomer's interactions and gain a comprehensive understanding of their values and conduct.

Moreover, this temporal buffer acts as a deterrent to those with ill intentions, serving notice that the community prioritizes the safety and well-being of its children. Potential wrongdoers are dissuaded by the robust and transparent vetting process, deterring any expedient attempts to exploit vulnerabilities within the system.

The six-month rule is a pragmatic and time-tested approach that reaffirms our commitment to creating a secure environment for the most vulnerable members of our faith community. It is not merely a temporal marker but a profound manifestation of our collective responsibility and dedication to fostering a space where children can flourish without compromising their safety.

Child Safety Policy

Churches that are serious about child protection will establish written policies for that explicit purpose. Having a policy in place will help to ensure the safety, well-being, and spiritual development of the youngest members within the church community. This is the way church leaders stand up for their most vulnerable. By implementing a policy, you are declaring your commitment to the principles of compassion and protection; you are also equipping your leaders with a guide on how to prevent and address instances of child neglect and abuse. There are many elements that your church could include in these policies; however, here are a few that should be included at a minimum.

1. A Clear Statement of Commitment: Begin with a concise and unequivocal statement that articulates the church's unwavering commitment to the safety and protection of children within its care. This declaration sets the tone for the entire policy, emphasizing the moral and spiritual imperative of safeguarding the vulnerable.

2. Definition of Child Abuse: Clearly define and elaborate what constitutes child abuse within the context of the church. This section should encompass various forms of abuse, including physical, emotional, and sexual, providing a comprehensive understanding for all stakeholders involved.

3. Screening and Selection Procedures: Outline meticulous procedures for the recruitment, screening, and selection of individuals who will work with children. Include background checks, reference verifications, and a thorough application process to ensure that individuals with a history of misconduct are identified and excluded from roles involving minors.

4. Training and Education: Develop a structured training program for all staff, volunteers, and leaders involved in children's ministry. This policy should lay out the frequency of training sessions and the topics to be covered. It should include but not be limited to recognizing signs of abuse, appropriate behavior with children, and the mandatory reporting of suspected abuse. Regular updates and refreshers should be incorporated to ensure ongoing awareness.

5. Supervision Guidelines: Establish clear guidelines for the supervision of children during church activities and events. Define appropriate adult-to-child ratios, delineate procedures for one-on-one interactions, and ensure that no child is left unsupervised at any time.

6. Reporting Procedures: Implement a straightforward and confidential reporting mechanism for suspicions or incidents of child abuse. Clearly articulate the steps to be taken, including reporting to designated authorities, internal reporting channels, and the involvement of law enforcement if necessary.

7. Response and Support: Develop a compassionate and supportive framework for responding to allegations of child abuse. This should include providing immediate support to the victim, initiating an internal investigation, and cooperating fully with external authorities. Clearly define consequences for individuals found guilty of abuse.

8. Communication Protocols: Establish clear communication protocols to disseminate the child protection policy to all stakeholders, including staff, volunteers, parents, and congregants. Regularly communicate updates and changes to ensure that everyone remains informed and engaged in the protection of children.

9. Physical Environment Safety: Ensure the physical safety of children by implementing measures such as secure check-in and check-out procedures, well-lit and monitored spaces, and regular safety inspections of facilities used for children's activities.

10. Confidentiality: Emphasize the importance of maintaining confidentiality in all matters related to child protection, balancing the need for transparency with the necessity of protecting the privacy of individuals involved.

A sample child protection policy is provided in Appendix 3 for you and your leadership team to adapt and customize. Be sure to consult an attorney, so they can provide expert legal feedback on the document.

By embracing these comprehensive elements within a child protection policy, churches not only fulfill their legal and moral obligations but also foster an environment where children can thrive, learn, and experience the love and care that is fundamental to the teachings of Christ. This policy becomes not just a document but a living testament to the church's commitment to protecting the most vulnerable members of its flock.

Codes of Conduct

A code of conduct is a set of guidelines and principles that outline the expected behavior, standards, and ethical considerations for individuals within a particular organization or community. It serves as a framework to guide the actions and interactions of members, emphasizing values, responsibilities, and expectations to maintain a safe, respectful, and inclusive environment. Codes of conduct are commonly utilized across various sectors, including business, educational, and religious institutions, to promote ethical conduct and define acceptable behavior.

Is there a Difference between a Code of Conduct and a Child Protection Policy?

To answer this question in a concise way, yes. There is a distinction between a code of conduct and a policy, although the terms are sometimes used interchangeably. Both are essential components of organizational governance, but they serve different purposes and have distinct characteristics.

A code of conduct is a set of principles, guidelines, and standards that articulate the expected behavior, values, and ethical standards for individuals within an organization. A code of conduct is often aspirational and may not delve into specific procedures or implementation details. Instead, it aims to establish a shared understanding of ethical behavior and the organization's values. While it sets expectations for behavior, it may not be as detailed or comprehensive as a policy.

Unlike a code of conduct, a policy is more concrete, providing detailed information about how the organization addresses certain issues, complies with regulations, and manages specific processes.

Policies are typically more specific, outlining the steps to be taken in various situations and the consequences for non-compliance. In the context of child protection, for instance, a church might have a child protection policy that outlines specific procedures for screening volunteers, reporting suspected abuse, and maintaining a safe environment. In summary, while both a code of conduct and a policy contribute to the overall governance of an organization, they serve different functions. A code of conduct focuses on overarching principles and values, setting a tone for ethical behavior, while a policy is more specific, outlining rules and procedures in detail to guide the organization's operations in various areas.

	Code of Conduct	Policy
Scope	Broad and focuses on ethical principles and values, setting the overall tone for behavior within an organization.	More specific, addressing areas of operation and providing detailed guidelines and procedures.
Level of Detail	Generally, less detailed and may not provide specific procedures for implementation.	More detailed, offering explicit instructions and steps to follow in various situations.
Aspiration vs. Implementation	Often aspirational, emphasizing ideals and values.	More practical, designed to guide behavior, decision-making, and operations.
Flexibility	Flexible and open to interpretation, allowing individuals to apply broad principles to their specific roles and responsibilities.	More rigid, providing clear guidelines that need to be followed consistently.

Importance of a Code of Conduct in Child Protection Programs at Churches

The code of conduct plays a crucial role in fostering a secure environment for children and youth. It also allows you to secure the signature of volunteers and employees, which is a declaration that they will uphold the conduct outlined in it. Here are several reasons why it is vital:

1. Establishing Expectations: A code of conduct clearly outlines the expectations for all individuals involved in the church community, including leaders, volunteers, staff, and congregants. This is essential for creating a shared understanding of appropriate behavior, especially concerning interactions with children.

2. Ensuring Child Safety: The primary goal of a child protection program is to ensure the safety and well-being of children. A code of conduct provides explicit guidelines on maintaining appropriate boundaries, preventing abuse, and promoting a culture of vigilance regarding child safety.

3. Preventing and Addressing Abuse: A well-crafted code of conduct includes provisions to prevent child abuse and offers a framework for reporting and addressing any concerns or suspicions of abuse. It provides clarity on what constitutes abusive behavior and emphasizes the duty to report such incidents promptly.

4. Setting Standards for Interactions: Child protection involves defining acceptable interactions between adults and children. The code of conduct delineates appropriate behaviors, communication methods, and physical contact, thereby minimizing the risk of misunderstandings or potential harm.

5. Guiding Adult and Youth Volunteers: For volunteers, both adults and youth, a code of conduct serves as a guide for appropriate behavior and interactions with children. It outlines the expectations for supervision, mentoring, and maintaining a safe environment during church-related activities.

6. Legal Compliance: A code of conduct ensures that the church complies with legal requirements and standards related to child protection. It helps to establish a proactive approach to child safety, which is crucial to meeting legal obligations and protecting the institution from legal liabilities.

7. Creating Accountability: By establishing clear expectations and consequences for violating the code of conduct, individuals within the church community become accountable for their actions. This accountability fosters a culture of responsibility and helps prevent misconduct.

8. Building Trust with Parents and Guardians: Parents and guardians entrust their children to the care of the church community. A robust code of conduct communicates the church's commitment to child protection, building trust among parents and encouraging their active involvement in the church's child safety initiatives.

A code of conduct serves as a foundational document in the child protection framework of churches, providing a roadmap for ethical behavior, preventing abuse, and ensuring the safety and well-being of the youngest members of the congregation. Its implementation is integral to creating a secure and nurturing environment where children can thrive spiritually, emotionally, and physically.

Check-in or Check-out Procedure

Establishing a robust check-in and check-out process for children left in the care of youth leaders is very important. This organized system acts as an effective line of defense, creating a secure environment that safeguards children from the risks associated with abduction. Whether parents or guardians check in their children manually or through electronic means, the church ensures that only authorized individuals gain access to designated areas while concurrently establishing a reliable record-keeping mechanism.

This meticulous approach not only minimizes the potential for unauthorized entry into children's programs but also provides a real-time attendance account, facilitating prompt identification during emergencies. In the church I attend, their system includes a camera that captures the image of the person dropping off the child, while it also records the time they were dropped off, along with the contact information for the parent.

Upon completion of the check-in process, parents receive a name tag for the child and a corresponding check-in slip, which is required for picking up the child. If an individual arrives without the slip or explicit parental authorization, efforts are made to contact the parent before releasing the child into their care. This is a very simple and effective way to ensure that we have a documented process for children that are in our care and custody. It is widely acknowledged by experts that this process is primarily applicable for children below the age of ten years old.

CHAPTER 13

Trust, Authority, and the Grooming Process

Camilla and her mother Gladys faced significant financial struggles after relocating to the US for a fresh start. Despite obtaining permanent residency through Camilla's grandmother, Gladys found it challenging to secure even part-time employment while pursuing an education to become a Licensed Practical Nurse. The financial strain on Camilla's grandmother eventually reached a breaking point, and she regretfully informed them they could no longer stay with her.

The pair began attending a nearby church, where Gladys, during a prayer meeting, vulnerably sought support for their dire circumstances and impending homelessness. The following day, the pastor visited them, offering not only spiritual solace but also a tangible lifeline. He linked them with a church member offering a one-bedroom rental, arranging for the church to cover the rent while Gladys completed her studies. Gladys was overwhelmed with gratitude toward the church community which seemed like a beacon of hope in their darkest times.

Initially, everything was looking up. The pastor regularly checked on them, often providing food from the church pantry, reinforcing Gladys's faith in the kindness of their new fellowship. However, this sense of security was soon shattered when Camilla confided in her mother, revealing discomfort in her interactions with the pastor. With reluctance, the truth emerged—what appeared to be pastoral care was a predatory grooming process by the pastor towards the fourteen-year-old.

The pastor, who had acquired Camilla's cell phone number under the pretense of a one-time arrangement to pick her up from school, had since initiated inappropriate communication. What started with benign biblical passages escalated to personal compliments and disturbing comments about her developing body. His instructions to Camilla to keep these exchanges hidden from Gladys were red flags of grooming behavior—feigning protection, seeking exclusivity, and attempting to earn undue trust.

Upon confronting the pastor with the evidence of his messages, his excuses were dismissals of innocence and deceitful denials. This discovery prompted Gladys to sever ties with the pastor and the church, and to decline further assistance despite their precarious situation.

This chilling example underscores the pernicious nature of grooming and the importance of open dialogue between children and guardians. Camilla's ability to express her discomfort to Gladys was critical in preventing further manipulation. This incident serves as a stark reminder that grooming behaviors pose a real danger within churches, often concealed under the guise of mentorship or spiritual guidance. It's a call to action—a need for education on the signs of grooming to protect the innocent and prevent entrapment in a devious cycle of abuse and misplaced guilt.

Church leaders such as pastors, administrators, and ministry leaders hold positions of authority. The inherent respect and trust associated with these roles can be exploited by perpetrators to gain access to and manipulate vulnerable children. Remember the wolf in sheep's clothing analogy? The behavior carried out by these individuals is seemingly innocent and could be mistaken as coming from a righteous place.

If there is significant focus on being aware of grooming within a faith-based community, this will reduce the odds of child sexual abuse at your church significantly. It is very important that your supervisors, parents, and children know how to spot grooming behaviors and to take action before the situation escalates.

Grooming behaviors can manifest in various ways and may be subtle or overt. It's crucial to stay vigilant and be aware of potential signs. While not exhaustive, the following list highlights some grooming behaviors that can occur in a church setting.

1. Excessive Attention: Groomers often target specific individuals and give them excessive, unwarranted attention. This may involve compliments, gifts, or an overemphasis on building a close relationship.

2. Isolation: Groomers may seek to isolate a child from their peers or adults by offering special privileges, attention, or opportunities. This isolation makes the child more vulnerable to manipulation.

3. Secrets and Special Relationships: Groomers often create secret relationships with children, asking them to keep secrets or share information that they don't want others to know. They may frame this secrecy to supposedly build trust.

4. Testing Boundaries: Groomers may gradually test and violate personal boundaries. This can start with seemingly innocent actions and escalate over time to more inappropriate or intrusive behavior.

5. Flattery and Emotional Manipulation: Groomers frequently use flattery and emotional manipulation to make a child feel special or valued. They may exploit vulnerabilities, seeking to create a sense of dependency.

6. Gifts and Favors: Offering gifts or special favors is a common grooming tactic. Groomers use these gestures to establish a sense of gratitude and obligation in the child.

7. Inappropriate Touch or Contact: Groomers may slowly introduce inappropriate physical contact, such as hugs, touches, or massages, under the guise of affection or care.

8. Online Exploitation: In the digital age, groomers may exploit online platforms to establish connections with children. This can include inappropriate messaging, sharing explicit content, or attempting to meet in person.

9. Undermining Authority: Groomers often seek to undermine the authority of parents, guardians, or other trusted adults in the child's life. They may try to position themselves as a more understanding or caring figure.

10. Groomer's Familiarity with Child Protection Policies: Some groomers may actively involve themselves in church activities, volunteering for roles that provide access to children. They may gain a detailed knowledge of the church's child protection policies to exploit any weaknesses.

It's important to note that these behaviors, when observed individually, may not necessarily indicate grooming. However, a pattern or combination of these behaviors, especially when coupled with secrecy and isolation, should raise concerns. Creating a culture of open communication and awareness within the church community is crucial for preventing and addressing grooming behaviors.

CHAPTER 14

Confronting the Culture of Silence

Some faith communities struggle with a culture of silence and a reluctance to address sensitive issues openly. Fear of tarnishing the reputation of the community or damaging the image of religious leaders can contribute to the underreporting of child sex abuse.

I once read about a case in which a beloved church elder was responsible for the abuse and molestation of more than twenty young ladies. Many of them were exposed to inappropriate touching during the prepubescent stage of their development. The survivors only became aware of the fact that his behavior was inappropriate as they matured. When one young lady shared some of the details of her abuse with a trusted adult, she was accused of being a liar and told never to repeat such baseless allegations again.

The fear of embarrassing this man was stronger than the commitment to the safety of this child. Sadly, this young lady's story is shared by so many other victims, some of whom now live with guilt and shame because they felt that they were somehow complicit with the predator who took advantage of their innocence. As a church officer, you can become a trusted ally to many, by breaking the culture of silence. Here are a few things you can do.

1. Take all allegations of abuse seriously. Too many stories have been told of children sharing horrible or inappropriate acts committed against them, but alas, they were not taken seriously.

2. Believe the victims. This is the first and most important factor in the process of breaking the culture of silence. We must create a safe space for those who are victims of abuse to report acts of abuse that have been committed against them.

3. Learn about the signs of abuse and be prepared to identify and act when you see them manifest in children who attend church.

4. Promote open dialogue with both adults and children, where those who "see something" can "say something."

5. Hold fellow leaders accountable to the established laws, policies and protocols concerning the handling of complaints.

6. Reportable offenses are to be reported to the agency responsible for the investigations, even if an internal investigation will take place.

Responding to an Allegation: Applying Accountability

In many cases, churches lack proper mechanisms for accountability and transparency. This is the perfect ecosystem for the wolves in sheep clothing to thrive and wreak havoc on their victims. Earlier we discussed the importance of establishing policies and procedures that will outline expectations and provide details on actions that will be taken when certain behaviors are present. In this section I will provide a few recommended steps on how you can bring accountability to life in your ministry organization.

1. Establish written policies and procedures that will speak directly to sexual misconduct and child sexual abuse. This policy should be used as part of the training process for all church leaders. It should have sections that address the handling of an allegation, how the church treats registered sex offenders, and the code of conduct for leaders.

2. Whenever a victim comes forward with a verbal complaint, it is important that you request that this person put their complaint in writing.

3. Upon receiving a complaint, verbal or written, the accused party should be placed on administrative leave and should be given an opportunity to respond to the complaint in writing.

4. If the offence is a police matter, law enforcement should be contacted immediately upon receipt of the information from the alleged victim. Please note that as a church, leaders have an ethical and sacred duty to corporate with law enforcement during their investigation.

5. Uphold the utmost confidentiality standards during the investigation. It is imperative that we adhere to the highest standards of confidentiality when handling incidents involving victims and accused parties. Limiting the dissemination of information to a select and essential group of individuals is paramount to mitigate potential adverse consequences for all involved parties. Failure to maintain this confidentiality may not only lead to detrimental effects on the individuals concerned but can also result in legal ramifications, including the pursuit of defamation lawsuits.

It is essential to acknowledge that in certain instances the victim or their family may choose to share details of the incident within the community. While this scenario is not ideal, it is crucial to recognize the limited control that church leadership may exercise in preventing such disclosures. The focal point, however, should be on those in leadership roles maintaining an unwavering commitment to the highest level of confidentiality.

Leadership must refrain from becoming the source of information dissemination. Acknowledging the potential challenges posed by external disclosures, church leaders must prioritize safeguarding the sensitive nature of incidents and refrain from contributing to the spread of information. In doing so, they not only protect the reputation and well-being of the individuals involved but also uphold the integrity of the institution amidst the complexities of incident management.

6. Handle all internal investigations in compliance with established protocols. As a leader within your faith community, you may never be able to prevent an incident from occurring at your church, and this will impact the level of exposure. However, the way an allegation is handled, could make all the difference between damages that rise to the level of negligence or gross negligence. If I may put this another way, it could be the difference between $100,000 and $27 million.

Legal and Reporting Challenges

Statute of Limitations: Legal challenges, including statutes of limitations, may hinder the prosecution of perpetrators. In some cases, survivors may not come forward until years later, and restrictive legal frameworks may limit their ability to seek justice.

Underreporting: Due to the stigma associated with child sex abuse and fear of retaliation, many cases go unreported. This underreporting makes it challenging to assess the true extent of the problem within faith communities.

Addressing the child sex abuse problem within communities of faith requires a concerted effort from religious leaders, community members, and external authorities. By fostering a culture of openness, accountability, and prioritizing the safety and well-being of children, faith communities can work towards preventing and addressing this deeply troubling issue.

CHAPTER 15

Personal Injury (Accident) Prevention

Accidents are an unfortunate reality of life, but when they occur in a sacred space like a church, the impact can be even more devastating. Church officers have a responsibility to prioritize the safety and well-being of everyone who associates with their churches. Taking proactive measures to minimize the likelihood of accidents is crucial in fulfilling this duty. In this chapter, we will explore the various steps that can be taken to prevent personal injury and ensure a safe environment for all.

From regular safety inspections to implementing proper maintenance and protocols, there are many ways to safeguard against accidents at church. When we take proactive steps to minimize accidents at church, we not only protect ourselves but also fulfill our sacred duty to care for others. Our actions can have a profound impact on the safety and well-being of our entire community. That is why it is essential to understand the risks and take necessary precautions to prevent accidents from occurring in the first place.

Slip, Trip, and Fall Accident Prevention

When preventing slip, trip, and fall accidents within a church setting, implementing a comprehensive strategy focused on safety and risk mitigation is crucial. Here is a list of measures a church can consider:

1. **Practice Regular Inspections:** Conduct routine inspections of the church premises to identify and promptly address potential slip, trip, and fall hazards. Pay close attention to high-traffic areas, entryways, and spaces frequently used by children and elderly members.

2. **Floor Maintenance:** Keep floors clean and dry, promptly cleaning up spills and addressing wet surfaces. Use appropriate warning signs when floors are being cleaned or are slippery.

3. **Non-Slip Surfaces:** Consider installing non-slip flooring or using slip-resistant mats in areas prone to wet conditions, such as entrances and restrooms.

4. **Proper Lighting:** Ensure that all areas are well-lit, particularly stairways, hallways, and entrances, to enhance visibility and reduce the risk of tripping over obstacles.

5. **Clear Walkways:** Keep walkways clear of clutter, furniture, or any obstacles that could obstruct the path and lead to tripping hazards.

6. Secure Rugs and Carpets: Use non-slip backing for rugs and carpets and secure them firmly to the floor to prevent tripping.

7. Handrails and Guardrails: Install handrails on staircases and ramps and ensure that guardrails are in place on elevated platforms to provide support and prevent falls.

8. Maintenance of Outdoor Spaces: Maintain outdoor areas, including parking lots and sidewalks, by promptly repairing any cracks or uneven surfaces that could pose tripping hazards.

9. Education and Awareness: Conduct safety training for staff and volunteers to raise awareness about slip, trip, and fall hazards. Encourage reporting of any potential hazards.

10. Footwear Guidelines: Encourage members and attendees to wear appropriate footwear, especially during adverse weather conditions.

11. Accessible Entrances: Ensure that entrances and exits are accessible and equipped with ramps or elevators for individuals with mobility challenges.

12. Snow and Ice Removal: Implement a snow and ice removal plan during winter months to prevent slippery surfaces in outdoor areas. It is also imperative that snow removals are documented in a log, recording the date and time as well as the name of the person that performed the task.

13. Emergency Preparedness: Develop and communicate emergency procedures for evacuations, ensuring that escape routes are clear and well-marked.

14. Childproofing Measures: Implement childproofing measures in areas frequented by children, including securing furniture and ensuring the absence of small objects that may cause tripping.

15. First Aid Stations: Maintain well-equipped first aid stations and ensure that staff or volunteers are trained in basic first aid to respond promptly to any injuries.

16. Reporting System: Establish a reporting system for members to report any hazards or concerns related to slip, trip, and fall risks. Investigation should be carried out on all reported cases of accidents and near misses. Though it is often overlooked, members should be encouraged to report near miss incidents as well.

By implementing these measures, a church can create a safer environment for its members and visitors, reducing the risk of slip, trip, and fall accidents within its premises.

Preventing Food Poisoning at Church Gatherings

At church events, the act of sharing meals takes center stage, fostering a sense of community and togetherness. But the importance of food safety is sometimes overlooked, and convenience often takes precedence. In faith-based communities where communal meals are a regular occurrence, prioritizing food safety is of utmost importance. This requires adherence to proper food handling, storage, and preparation practices.

To safeguard the health of attendees, it is crucial to designate trained individuals who can oversee and enforce food safety measures. These individuals play a pivotal role in ensuring that health and hygiene guidelines are consistently followed during the preparation and serving of meals. Additionally, conducting regular inspections of kitchen facilities is essential to identify and address potential hazards promptly.

By establishing a proactive approach to food safety within the church community, we can minimize the risk of foodborne illnesses and create an environment where shared meals can be enjoyed without concerns about health and safety.

Emphasizing Safety for Organized Trips and Activities

To establish a comprehensive safety framework for organized trips and activities, it is imperative to delve into key components such as conducting thorough risk assessments, prioritizing transportation safety, and having well-structured emergency plans in place.

Risk assessments serve as a proactive measure to identify potential hazards and assess the level of risk associated with various aspects of the trip or activity. By systematically analyzing potential dangers, organizers can implement preventive measures and contingency plans to mitigate risks effectively.

Transportation safety is a critical consideration, encompassing various facets such as vehicle maintenance, driver qualifications, and adherence to traffic regulations. Ensuring that transportation arrangements align with safety standards significantly contributes to the overall well-being of participants during the journey to and from the activity location.

Having robust emergency plans is a non-negotiable aspect of trip and activity safety. These plans should outline clear procedures for handling unforeseen events, medical emergencies, or any unexpected circumstances that may arise. The effectiveness of these plans relies on thorough communication, ensuring that all participants are aware of procedures and contact points in case of emergencies.

Clear communication extends to providing participants with detailed guidelines, outlining expected behavior, safety protocols, and any specific rules relevant to the activity. Equipping participants with this information promotes a collective understanding and commitment to safety measures, reducing the likelihood of accidents.

In addition to clear guidelines, having trained personnel overseeing activities is instrumental in maintaining a secure environment. These individuals should possess the expertise to respond swiftly and effectively in case of emergencies, further enhancing the overall safety of the trip or event. For example, have someone who is trained in first aid and CPR, and take along with you a well-stocked first-aid kit.

The meticulous attention to detail in risk assessments, transportation safety, emergency planning, clear communication, and trained supervision collectively forms a robust safety framework for organized trips and activities. Prioritizing these actions not only mitigates potential risks but also fosters an environment where participants can engage in enriching experiences with confidence and peace of mind.

Swimmer Safety

Going on church-sponsored trips is one of the things I looked forward to most at church during my own childhood years, especially those trips that involved water-based activities like swimming, snorkeling, canoeing, or surfing. However, as with summer camps, there are potential dangers that must be considered and prepared for in advance.

It is important to recognize that not all children have the same level of skill and experience in the water. As a trip organizer, it is your responsibility to ensure the safety of each participant and meet them at their individual level. Here are three swimming levels with corresponding measures.

1. Non-swimmers: For non-swimmers, primarily children under the age of seven or those who cannot demonstrate basic skills, extra attention and protection are required. These individuals should stay in shallow wading areas.

2. Intermediate: Intermediate swimmers, who can perform basic strokes but cannot swim long distances or stay afloat independently, should also remain in areas where they can comfortably stand.

3. Qualified swimmers: Qualified swimmers can confidently swim using different strokes, tread water, float on their backs for an extended period and enter and exit the water with ease. While these individuals still require supervision from a lifeguard, they can be given more freedom to swim and move around in deeper water.

To ensure the safety of all participants during water-based activities, it is critical to have a written protocol in place that guides staff members on proper lifeguarding techniques, supervision strategies, and the use of a buddy system. Additionally, it is important to have a plan in place to keep track of all individuals during swimming excursions to prevent any potential accidents or injuries. By prioritizing safety and proactively preparing for potential risks, church trips can provide enjoyable and safe swimming experiences for all participants.

Transportation Safety

When it comes to transportation safety, churches cannot afford to ignore the risks. In fact, data shows that transportation-related incidents are one of the leading causes of injuries and fatalities among churches and other nonprofit organizations.

According to the National Safety Council, motor vehicle crashes are the leading cause of death for individuals aged one to fifty-four in the United States.[1] In 2019, there were an estimated 38,800 fatalities and 4.4 million injuries from motor vehicle crashes. While it is unclear how many of these incidents involved churches or other nonprofit organizations, it is safe to say that transportation safety is a critical concern for these groups.

Furthermore, the costs of transportation-related incidents can be significant. In addition to direct costs such as vehicle repairs and medical bills, there are indirect costs such as lost productivity, legal fees, and damage to the organization's reputation. Large settlements and judgments resulting from transportation-related incidents have been known to bankrupt organizations, thus emphasizing the importance of mitigating these risks through comprehensive transportation safety programs.

As a church leader, it is your responsibility to ensure the safety of your congregation, employees, volunteers, and guests when traveling to and from church-related activities. Implementing a formal transportation safety program can help minimize your organization's exposure to liability and keep your people safe.

Church Mutual Insurance Company[2] recommends ten essential activities that can reduce the impact and likelihood of a transportation-related incident.

1. A driver program that includes defensive driving training and evaluation.

2. Implement proper vehicle selection and maintenance.

3. Ensure proper driver selection by reviewing driving records from the Department of Motor Vehicles.

4. Determine if a driver uses medication that may impair their ability to operate a motor vehicle.

5. Impeccable record-keeping that documents vehicle maintenance dates.

6. Regular vehicle inspections.

7. Perform risk assessments for upcoming trips (routes, weather, distance, etc.).

8. Develop a reporting system for incidents and near misses.

9. Provide emergency equipment on vehicles (fire extinguishers and other tools).

10. Establish a cellphone use policy.

While it may seem daunting to implement a comprehensive transportation safety program, the costs of not doing so can be catastrophic. Protect your church and those you serve by prioritizing transportation safety and implementing a program that covers all ten of these essentials.

CHAPTER 16

Employment Practices

Faith-based communities encounter similar challenges to those confronted by secular organizations in employment practices. From on-the-job injuries such as accidents, electrocution, and accidental dismemberment to broader concerns such as wrongful termination, harassment, and discrimination, safeguards are needed to preserve the safety and well-being of their employees.

Establishing effective safeguards becomes crucial for churches to diminish the probability of such occurrences or to mitigate their impact on the overall functioning of the religious institution. How can a church strategically implement the necessary measures to achieve this objective? I submit to you that practicing sound risk management is one of the foremost tools within the arsenal of church leaders to combat these challenges.

The point has been well established, but it cannot be overstated: The sanctity of religious organizations does not shield them from the complexities of the modern world. In fact, the very essence of their communal nature amplifies the need for thoughtful and deliberate approaches to risk management in the area of employment practices. The individuals who form the backbone of these communities—clergy, administrators, volunteers, and staff—constitute a rich mosaic of talents and backgrounds. As with any diverse and dynamic group, the potential for challenges, conflicts, and uncertainties looms large.

This chapter endeavors to explore, dissect, and illuminate the multifaceted ways in which risk management considerations intersect with employment practices within communities of faith. From hiring and training to conflict resolution and crisis response, each facet of personnel management holds implications for the vitality and resilience of these sacred gatherings. Moreover, the inherent responsibility to safeguard the well-being of congregants and community members adds layers of complexity to the stewardship of human resources within religious organizations.

How does the subject of sound employment practices keep your church out of the courts? We will look at several factors such as legal compliance, ethical considerations, ministerial exception, and the delicate balance between nurturing a spiritually enriching environment and safeguarding against potential pitfalls. Through real-world examples and practical insights, you will be equipped as a church officer, administrator, or stakeholder with the tools necessary to navigate the intricate landscape of employment practices with wisdom and foresight.

We will take a deep dive into the heart of faith-based employment dynamics, recognizing that effective risk management is not a compromise of sacred values but rather an affirmation of the commitment to the well-being and flourishing of the entire community. As we explore this crucial topic, may we be guided by the understanding that the path to resilient and thriving communities of faith is paved with the intentional and conscientious management of risks inherent in the human experience.

Personnel Management

In the quiet sanctity of an old country church, tragedy unfolded as Brother Stanley, a revered sixty-five-year-old deacon, embarked on a perilous journey to repair the gutters on the roof. His impatience, ignited by the absence of his spotter, Brother Brown, pushed him to defy safety protocols and ascend the ladder alone.

The sun-drenched afternoon witnessed a fateful decision that would alter the course of Brother Stanley's life. The ladder, seemingly secure on an even surface, transformed into an instrument of catastrophe. As he stretched to reach an unreachable spot, the ladder succumbed to the laws of physics, careening sideways and sending Brother Stanley into a harrowing descent.

The aftermath was silent but devastating. Unconscious and unable to summon aid, Brother Stanley lay undiscovered. The consequences were severe—extensive brain injuries that rendered him incapacitated.

This tragic incident serves as a haunting reminder that safety is not an option but an imperative. Church employees, like their counterparts in any profession, face a myriad of hazards that can shatter lives and ministries. The question looms: How do we fortify our houses of worship with the armor of best practices to shield against such life-altering calamities?

Like the sacred Scriptures themselves, the art of personnel management in a church requires careful consideration and implementation of principles that safeguard the well-being of those who serve. While the subject is vast and nuanced, a glimpse into key activities can illuminate the path toward effective personnel management. Brother Stanley's story serves as a reminder, beckoning us to not only reflect on the importance of safety but also to engrave it into the very fabric of our ministry.

Strategies for Effective Personnel Management

In addressing the top risks facing communities of faith in the realm of employment practices, here are a few things they should have in place to be in the strongest position possible in order to prevent costly lawsuits and high turnover rates and to increase productivity:

1. Develop and update policies for personnel and volunteers.
2. Hire, inspire, and fire with excellence.
3. Invest in training and development.
4. Know the law.

Develop and Update Policies

If you haven't caught on yet, by now you should realize that having written policies in place is quite essential to the risk management processes of a church, especially in the areas of human resource management. Some of the key areas that your policies should address include:

- Hiring
- Termination
- Discipline
- Discrimination and harassment
- Employee benefits
- Conflict of interest
- Leave
- Overall code of conduct

When developing policies, it is imperative that subject matter experts in the areas of law, human resources, and risk management be enlisted to serve on committees. Involving these experts early in the process will help to save time and resources when developing a policy framework to withstand the test of legal rigor.

It should also be noted that policies should go through the established process to be regarded as official. For some entities, policies are not considered valid unless they are ratified by a board of governors.

A friend of mine who works for a very large church organization related a very interesting experience to me. The human resource director established a committee to develop a code of conduct to address a specific challenge faced by certain employee groups. Once the committee finalized the document, the HR director proceeded to disseminate it to all affected employees for signature, failing to follow established protocols. The document threatened to terminate employees who failed to sign it by a specific deadline.

One employee refused to sign the document, leading to a challenge of its validity. The employee prevailed because the document was not established as official policy by the board of governors. The incident could have caused a great deal of legal problems for the organization.

Treat Policies as Live Documents

It's essential for organizations to view policies as live documents that can be updated to reflect the ever-evolving social, legal, political, religious, and ethical landscape. The purpose is to keep policies relevant, accurate, and effective for employees. As is the case with newly established policies, updated policies are to go through the same process, ensuring compliance. This process is crucial to avoid confusion, legal issues, and a negative impact on employee morale and productivity.**Hire, Inspire, and Fire with Excellence**

Given the important role that employees play in contributing to the overall success of religious organizations, imperatives of hiring, inspiring, and firing with excellence are paramount considerations that transcend mere administrative functions. Operating within an environment where faith intertwines with governance, the significance of these actions becomes amplified, shaping not only the internal dynamics of the church but also its external influence on the broader community.

Incorporating risk management perspective within the overall talent strategy at church is not just prudent; it is a strategic necessity. The complex decisions related to recruitment, termination, and motivation within a religious context must align with the overarching goal of safeguarding the spiritual well-being of the congregation, while fortifying the institutional integrity. This next section explores the critical importance of approaching these personnel-related matters with an expert risk management lens, ensuring that the hiring, firing, and inspiring processes resonate with excellence, accountability, and a steadfast commitment to the core values of the faith community.

Hiring with Excellence

Whether considering the prospect of hiring a senior or junior pastor, or even a musician for the praise team, the process of hiring personnel in communities of faith is one that requires meticulous attention and a strategic approach. The significance of selecting individuals to serve within the sacred framework of a faith community extends far beyond conventional employment practices. Each appointment is not just a staffing decision; it is a commitment to upholding the spiritual integrity of the congregation and navigating the intricate dynamics of a religious community.

The act of hiring in this context involves not only identifying skills and qualifications but also assessing the potential impact the hiring decision will have on the sacred mission and values of the church and the culture of the team and organization. In the following sections, we will explore measures that a church or faith-based organization can take to minimize risks associated with hiring.

The Importance of Background Screening

Upon receiving a female as his associate, Pastor White was initially elated, despite the prevailing issues surrounding gender dynamics in ministry. Confident in his congregation's progressive stance on this matter, he warmly embraced her arrival, and they collaborated seamlessly during the initial phase of her tenure.

While Pastor White had a role on the interview panel, he was not intricately involved in the identification and subsequent screening process that led to her appointment in the role. Unfortunately, their rapport soured after the associate pastor interpreted some of her first performance feedback in a very negative way.

Following the meeting, she started spreading detrimental rumors about Pastor White among some of the most influential members, causing a significant rift in the church. The damage was substantial, with approximately 20 percent of these members departing never to return to that congregation. Further investigation revealed a negative track record on her part that diligent background screening could have easily uncovered prior to her selection.

This incident highlights the importance of examining not only overt qualifications like transcripts and work experience but also behavioral factors during the candidate assessment process. Some organizations utilize behavioral assessment tools such as DiSC, Myers Briggs, Gallup Strength Finders, or the Predictive Index, alongside institutional reference checks that are listed on resumés. It underscores the importance of digging into a candidate's work history, recognizing that behavior is a much more reliable predictor of success in faith communities than solely relying on the education and experience listed on a resumé.

Implement Transparent Hiring Practices

Depending on the structure of your organization, hiring may be handled from a centralized location, or it might be done at a local entity that has designated hiring managers for the role in question. Regardless of the structure of your church or organization, it is imperative that a very open and transparent process be implemented.

This is a very extensive subject, but here are three things you can do to support a transparent hiring process.

1. Clearly Defined Job Descriptions: Initiate transparency by providing clear and comprehensive job descriptions. Clearly outline the responsibilities, qualifications, and expectations associated with the position to ensure that prospective candidates have a thorough understanding of the role.

2. Open Communication Channels: Establish open lines of communication throughout the hiring process. Communicate key milestones, timelines, and any changes in the process to both internal and external stakeholders. Respond promptly to inquiries and provide feedback to candidates, reinforcing a culture of transparency and openness.

3. Inclusive Decision-making: Involve relevant stakeholders, such as other church leaders, staff members, and key volunteers, in the decision-making process. It is quite easy for things like nepotism to seep into the hiring process. The way to guard against this is to embrace diversity among key members within the church leadership and community to evaluate and interview potential candidates.

Inspiring with Excellence

Cultivating an environment where employees and volunteers are not only present but fully engaged is essential for the success of the ministry. While some religious organizations may overlook the importance of investing in the training and development of their key personnel, wise church leaders understand that such investment pays dividends in the long run.

One impactful approach is to establish a performance management system that facilitates the growth and progress of individuals within the organization. This involves setting clear goals, providing constructive feedback, and recognizing achievements.

Additionally, creating an inspiring work environment is paramount. This can be achieved through small yet meaningful gestures, such as expressing gratitude, fostering a culture of collaboration, and recognizing the unique contributions of each team member.

Even in the absence of an extensive budget for offsite retreats, leaders can invest in simple actions like team-building activities, regular check-ins, and providing opportunities for skill development. These efforts not only enhance the overall engagement of the team but also contribute significantly to the success of the ministry, aligning the collective efforts with the shared vision and mission of the faith community.

Firing with Excellence: Safeguarding Organizations through Effective Termination Practices

The process of terminating an employee from a faith-based organization requires the utmost compassion and empathy, recognizing the challenging and complex nature of this situation. When the culture of the church is one in which there is substantial alignment between the values and behaviors of employees, it is uncommon for terminations to occur. But when the situation warrants a termination, it is crucial to approach it with a caring and nurturing attitude. Church environments thrive on the principles of love and goodwill, and it is critical to extend these virtues to employees during the termination process.

Sometimes when engaged in the process of termination, leaders tend to compartmentalize their faith, allowing their emotions rather than their faith to lead their decision-making.

It is important to acknowledge that termination is a traumatic and disruptive experience. Many individuals may find their sense of purpose and belonging within the church, and the loss of their employment may be like losing a part of their identity. As leaders, we must understand the employees' need to be heard and respected during this process. They should be provided with a compassionate, empathetic, and dignified exit strategy, despite the challenging nature of the situation.

The importance of making terminations as amicable as possible cannot be overstated, as it can minimize the impact on the church community. A poorly executed termination can create ripples of negativity among the remaining employees and ultimately tarnish the reputation of the organization. As such, the leaders need to enforce ethical and professional practices when dealing with any termination process. Leaders must be transparent, explaining their decisions in a clear and concise manner, and showing empathy, compassion, and goodwill as much as possible.

Moreover, it is essential to acknowledge that a loss of income can be a significant challenge for employees facing terminations. As leaders of the church organization, we must ensure that we provide relevant support, including financial assistance where possible, to ensure that the terminated employees can transition out of their role within the church organization with minimum friction. Doing so is paramount in ensuring that employees feel seen, heard, and cared for even post-termination.

So how does one fire with excellence? Following are some of the most critical steps that should be taken as part of the termination process.

1. *Legal Compliance:* One of the primary reasons for prioritizing excellent termination practices is ensuring legal compliance. Terminating an employee in a manner that aligns with employment laws and regulations minimizes the risk of legal challenges and associated liabilities.

2. *Clear Policies and Procedures:* Establishing clear termination policies and procedures provides a framework for consistency and fairness. When employees understand the criteria and processes for termination, it fosters transparency, reduces ambiguity, and lowers the risk of disputes.

3. *Documentation:* Thorough documentation of the termination process is a key component of risk reduction. Keeping detailed records of performance issues, disciplinary actions, and the termination decision itself can serve as valuable evidence in the event of a legal challenge.

4. *Consistent Communication:* Communicating termination decisions consistently and professionally is crucial. Clear and compassionate communication helps employees understand the reasons behind their termination. This minimizes the likelihood of misinterpretation or resentment that could lead to legal action.

5. Training for Managers: Providing training for managers on effective termination practices is an investment in risk mitigation. Equipping managers with the skills to handle terminations respectfully and within legal bounds contributes to a smoother process and reduces the likelihood of legal repercussions.

6. Exit Interviews: Conducting exit interviews can provide valuable insights into employees' perspectives and experiences. It serves not only as an opportunity for feedback but also as a proactive measure to address potential concerns before they escalate into legal challenges.

7. Review and Update Policies: Regularly reviewing and updating termination policies in accordance with evolving employment laws ensures ongoing compliance. Staying abreast of legal changes helps organizations adapt their practices to minimize legal risks.

8. Seek Legal Counsel: In cases of complex terminations or uncertainty about legal obligations, seeking legal counsel is a prudent step. Legal professionals can provide guidance on navigating termination processes, which reduces the likelihood of legal challenges.

9. Confidentiality Measures: Implementing confidentiality measures during and after the termination process is essential. Protecting sensitive information and maintaining confidentiality can prevent reputational damage and legal complications.

10. Consider Alternative Resolutions: Exploring alternative resolutions, such as mediation or severance agreements, can sometimes provide amicable solutions that mitigate the risk of legal action. These alternatives showcase an organization's commitment to fairness and resolution, while also safeguarding the church from future legal liability.

In my years of serving faith-based organizations, I have yet to see one employment practices claim that ended up before a jury. Ninety percent of these cases have been settled with significant sums paid out to disgruntled former employees. While lawsuits are, many times, out of the control of employers, the actions taken during the termination process can minimize the risks. Firing with excellence is not merely procedural; it is a strategic risk management decision. By prioritizing legal compliance, clear communication, documentation, and ongoing policy updates, organizations can significantly reduce the risk of wrongful termination lawsuits. This reflects a workplace environment that values fairness, transparency, and compliance.

CHAPTER 17

Ministerial Exception (Exemption)

Religious organizations stand in a unique legal landscape when it comes to employment practices, particularly in the United States of America. Civil courts typically avoid entangling themselves with internal church governance and doctrinal matters; they acknowledge a need for deference to religious autonomy. This is where the ministerial exception—an important legal doctrine in United States employment law—comes into play. Ministerial exception means that the government stays out of hiring and any kind of dispute regarding qualified religious leaders and their religious employers, like churches or religious schools.

The ministerial exception has its roots in the First Amendment of the U.S. Constitution, which bars the government from interfering with a church's freedom of religion, effectively allowing religious bodies autonomy in their internal decisions, particularly concerning who can and cannot be a minister.

Key Legal Precedence: Hosanna-Tabor v. E.E.O.C.

The landmark case of *Hosanna-Tabor Evangelical Lutheran Church and School v. Equal Employment Opportunity Commission*, 132 S.Ct. 694 (2012), serves as a vital touchstone for religious entities. In this case, the Supreme Court's unanimous decision confirmed that the ministerial exception barred an employment discrimination lawsuit brought by a "called" teacher, underscoring not just the distinction granted to ministers but also indicating a broader application that may encompass other religious roles.

The ministerial exception was definitively acknowledged, indicating that religious institutions are granted autonomy to decide on matters integral to their spiritual missions without the constraints typically imposed by employment discrimination laws.[1]

Hiring and Firing: A Religious Organization's Conundrum

Church leaders often face complex decisions when hiring and firing ministers—balancing the preservation of religious values with fair employment practices. Here are some hypothetical scenarios illustrative of the gray areas church leaders might navigate.

1. Consideration of Personal Beliefs: If a minister professes a belief or adopts a lifestyle that diverges from those held by the church, leadership faces the difficult decision of whether such differences merit termination, or if they fall within acceptable bounds of individual expression. Churches must tread carefully, considering both legal implications and community expectations.

2. Conflict with Church Doctrine: Should a minister publicly dispute key church doctrines or act in ways that contradict them, leaders must decide how to reconcile the individual's religious freedom with the congregation's doctrinal consistency. The gravity of doctrinal adherence against the spectrum of permissible beliefs must be judiciously weighed.

3. Faith-Related Employment Conditions: Asking potential ministers to agree to specific credal affirmations is commonplace in faith-based hires. However, leaders must be clear on which beliefs and practices are essential to the role. Detailed job descriptions and contracts can help clarify these conditions from the outset.

Balancing Act: Walking the Line of Legal and Spiritual Obligations

Given the protection afforded by the ministerial exception, church leaders have substantial latitude to operate according to their religious convictions. Nonetheless, it is prudent to adopt practices that both honor the spirit of employment law and reinforce the integrity of their religious mission, such as:

1. Clear Job Descriptions: Articulate the religious significance and requirements of ministerial roles, delineating the expectations and grounds upon which employment decisions will be made.

2. Documented Policies: Maintain comprehensive, written policies relating to hiring, conduct, discipline, and dismissal, clearly grounded in the religious precepts of the organization.

3. Consistent Application: Apply policies uniformly to avoid any appearance of discrimination or arbitrary decision-making, which may provide grounds for litigation.

4. Training and Education: Regularly train leadership and administrative personnel on the nuances of the ministerial exception and legal best practices for employment issues.

5. Seek Legal Counsel: Engage with legal counsel sensitive to religious and employment law to navigate ambiguous situations and ensure compliance with legal standards.

While the ministerial exception affords churches wide discretion in managing their ministers, carrying out employment practices with clear guidelines, transparency, fairness, and a commitment to the religious tenets of the organization remains paramount. By doing so, church leaders can safeguard their religious prerogatives while fostering an environment of respect and dignity.

Potential Lawsuits Despite the Exception

Even with the safety net of the ministerial exception, navigating employment decisions requires delicate judgment. Church authorities must understand that while this protection exists, it isn't an invulnerable shield against all forms of litigation.

In cases where the termination or hiring decision isn't transparently related to the religious tenets of the church or appears retaliatory, the risk of legal action looms larger. It's a reminder that while the ministerial exception extends a broad covering, it is neither absolute nor simplistic. The challenge unfolds when the reasons for an employment decision hover in a zone that is not evidently tied to religion or seem to be retaliatory rather than doctrinal.

A common pitfall for church leadership is the failure to communicate clearly how the employment decision connects to their spiritual governance. This can open the door to lawsuits, as courts may find it challenging to discern the religious from the secular in the absence of express reasoning in the church's actions.

To mitigate potential legal challenges, there is prudence in churches documenting how their employment decisions relate to and uphold the church's doctrines. However, even meticulous records can sometimes be insufficient. This is especially true when the situation involves accusations of discrimination or retaliation that seem secular in nature and therefore potentially fall outside the protection of the ministerial exception.

Consulting with Legal Counsel

When the waters of employment practices become murky, seeking legal counsel becomes indispensable for church leaders. Lawyers well-versed in constitutional and employment law can provide clarity and guide churches through the labyrinth of hiring and firing within the bounds of both church doctrine and civil law.

Legal professionals can:

- Help navigate the grey areas and vulnerabilities that exist despite the ministerial exception.
- Advise on crafting clear employment policies that are doctrinally sound and legally defensible.
- Aid in properly documenting employment decisions in anticipation of potential disputes.

As church leaders navigate the challenges associated with managing their ministerial teams, they tread on a complex blend of sacred duty and secular law. The guiding light through this terrain is a nuanced understanding of the ministerial exception, a commitment to upholding the religious mission authentically and transparently, and the wisdom to enlist legal support when necessary. It's a journey requiring both legal insight and spiritual discernment, ensuring that each step taken is both legally sound and faith aligned.

CHAPTER 18

Creating a Safe Environment through Sound Ergonomic Practices

Allowing employees to feel that they work in a safe environment goes a very long way in improving workplace dynamics, productivity, and reducing the risk of on-the-job injury. One often-neglected area is workplace ergonomics.

Ergonomics involves designing and arranging the workplace to fit the capabilities and limitations of the individuals working there. This not only enhances efficiency and productivity but, more importantly, mitigates the risk of musculoskeletal disorders and other health issues associated with poor ergonomics.

Faith-based organizations can be a hub of activity, with a range of tasks conducted by people of different ages, sizes, and abilities. Tasks such as lifting, carrying, sitting, standing, and typing can lead to musculoskeletal disorders if not conducted safely and with proper ergonomic practices.

This chapter will provide an overview of ergonomics in faith-based organizations, highlighting the benefits of implementing ergonomic practices and techniques to ensure safety, as well as offering practical solutions and tips for specific activities.

Benefits of Ergonomic Practices in Faith-based Organizations

1. Enhance safety and reduces risks of injury: One of the primary benefits of adopting ergonomic practices in faith-based organizations is to enhance safety and reduce the risk of injury. When people are performing tasks that require them to assume awkward postures, exert a lot of force, or repeat the same motions frequently, they are more susceptible to musculoskeletal disorders. The use of ergonomic practices such as proper lifting techniques, adjustable seating, and workstation positioning can minimize these risks and create a safer environment for employees and volunteers.

2. Increase productivity and efficiency: Ergonomic practices can also lead to increased productivity and efficiency within faith-based organizations. When staff and volunteers are comfortable and not distracted by aches and pains, they are able to focus better on their tasks, resulting in fewer errors and faster work completion. Proper ergonomic practices can also promote better collaboration and team dynamics, as individuals are more comfortable and able to interact with one another more effectively.

3. Enhance the overall well-being and health of individuals: Implementing ergonomic practices within faith-based organizations can also lead to enhanced well-being and health among individuals. Poor ergonomics practices can lead to chronic pain, discomfort, and stress, which can impact individuals' mental and physical health. By promoting proper ergonomic practices such as stretching, posture correction, and healthy movement habits, individuals can experience reduced stress and improved overall health and well-being.

Practical Solutions and Tips for Ergonomic Practices

Lifting and Carrying: Many tasks within faith-based organizations involve lifting and carrying items such as chairs, musical equipment, or books. When lifting and carrying items, individuals should follow proper techniques such as:
1. Bending the knees and keeping the back straight.
2. Holding the load close to the body.
3. Avoiding twisting movements while carrying.
4. Using carts or dollies to minimize the need to carry heavy items.

Sitting and Standing: Many tasks within faith-based organizations require individuals to sit or stand for extended periods. When sitting or standing, individuals should:

1. Keep their feet flat on the ground or footrest.
2. Use an adjustable chair with back support.

3. Take breaks and move around to reduce static postures.
4. Use standing desks to prevent prolonged sitting and to alleviate back pain.

Computer Workstation: Many faith-based organizations involve tasks that require individuals to work at a computer. When working at a computer, individuals should:

1. Position monitors at eye level.
2. Use an adjustable chair with lumbar support.
3. Keep their arms and wrists straight while typing.
4. Take breaks to stretch and move around.
5. Use ergonomic keyboards, mouses, and monitor arms.

Manual Handling: In churches where manual handling is prevalent, whether it be lifting, carrying, or moving objects, it's essential to educate employees and volunteers about proper techniques. Implement training programs to teach proper lifting and carrying methods, emphasizing the use of equipment like dollies or carts when handling heavy loads. Encourage frequent breaks to prevent fatigue and overexertion.

Ergonomic practices play a vital role in ensuring the safety, health, and well-being of individuals within faith-based organizations. By implementing proper ergonomic techniques such as lifting and carrying, sitting and standing, and computer workstation practices, individuals can avoid musculoskeletal disorders, increase productivity and efficiency, and enhance their overall health and well-being.

CHAPTER 19

Rendering Unto Caesar: The Importance of Legal Compliance

Compliance with the laws of the land is a fundamental requirement for every individual and institution. However, the relationship between church and state can often be complex and contentious. As religious institutions, churches have the responsibility to obey the laws of the state while also upholding their faith-based principles and beliefs.

This is a dilemma that has been faced for centuries, even by Jesus and the Pharisees themselves. In the biblical account of the payment of taxes, the Pharisees sought to trap Jesus in a question that demanded a compromising answer. They asked Him whether it was lawful to pay taxes to Caesar, knowing that Jews despised Roman rule and taxation. Jesus, with His profound wisdom and understanding of human nature, responded, "Give to Caesar what belongs to Caesar, and give to God what belongs to God." (Matthew 22:21)

This statement has been interpreted in various ways throughout history, but its essence remains a crucial lesson for all. When we are faced with a decision that requires us to either follow our conscience or comply with the law, we should always seek to find a balance between the two. Jesus' response implied that we can fulfill our obligations to the state without compromising our duties towards God.

Legal compliance can be considered a moral duty for Christians and other religious adherents. They must follow the laws of the land *if* those laws do not conflict with God's laws or their conscience. In doing so, they can ensure that their actions are in alignment with their faith-based values while also contributing toward the greater good of society at large.

The importance of legal compliance cannot be understated, especially in today's world, where the line between right and wrong is often blurred. This is why the encounter between Jesus and the Pharisees about the payment of taxes serves as a timely reminder that the decision to comply or not to comply with the law should never be taken lightly.

There are state and federal laws that govern workforce management. It is incumbent upon faith-based leaders to learn the applicable laws for their jurisdiction and do everything in their power to ensure compliance. There are several areas to consider under legal compliance.

Equal Employment Opportunity (EEO) Compliance

The concept of preferential hiring within religious organizations stands as a unique and often debated facet. The intertwining of faith and work raises questions about the balance between religious freedom and equal opportunity. It is a terrain where the boundaries of personal conviction and professional requirements are tested.

One of the distinctive aspects of religious organizations is the degree of autonomy they are granted when it comes to hiring practices. In many jurisdictions, laws exist that carve out exceptions for religious institutions, allowing them to consider an individual's religious beliefs when making employment decisions. This preferential treatment is rooted in the recognition of the vital role that faith plays in the identity and mission of these organizations.

In the United States, for example, Title VII of the Civil Rights Act of 1964 provides a religious exemption that allows religious organizations to give preference to individuals who share their faith. This exemption is a reflection of the constitutional principles of religious freedom and the understanding that a religious institution's ability to select employees who align with its beliefs is essential to the free exercise of religion.

Balancing Faith and Fairness

While the legal framework may provide leeway for religious organizations, the ethical considerations of preferential hiring warrant careful examination. Striking a balance between religious freedom and the principle of equal opportunity is a delicate task. Critics argue that such exemptions may perpetuate discrimination and undermine the broader societal commitment to fair and inclusive employment practices.

On the other hand, proponents contend that religious organizations serve a unique purpose in society, often driven by deeply held convictions and values. The ability to hire individuals who share these convictions is viewed as integral to maintaining the organization's identity and mission. For example, a church seeking to hire a pastor will find it essential to select an individual who aligns with the doctrinal tenets of the organization.

Navigating Diversity

The challenge for religious organizations lies in navigating the delicate balance between preserving their identity and fostering diversity. Many religious traditions emphasize the importance of welcoming all individuals, regardless of their background, into their communities. This inclusivity is often central to the teachings and principles of Christianity outlined in Matthew 28:19 to "go and make disciples of all the nations."

To navigate these complex waters, some religious organizations adopt nuanced approaches. They may prioritize faith alignment for certain roles directly involved in the spiritual leadership or doctrinal teaching, while promoting diversity in other areas such as administration, outreach, and community service.

Preferential hiring within religious organizations is a multifaceted issue that reflects the intricate interplay between religious freedom, organizational identity, and societal expectations. As individuals and institutions grapple with these dynamics, a nuanced understanding of the legal, ethical, and practical dimensions is essential. The challenge remains: how can religious organizations maintain their unique character while upholding principles of faith?

Anti-discrimination and Harassment Policies

Anti-discrimination and harassment policies are not only a legal and ethical imperative for church leaders, but also a reflection of the core values that underpin religious values. These policies are not just safeguards against legal liabilities; they are the armor that protects the sanctity of the community, fostering an environment where the principles of love, respect, and equality are upheld in every interaction.

In addition to the establishment of written policies, it is also crucial that employees are trained on these policies as well as part of the annual leaders/officers training planned by your church. In my years of being a risk manager, I have come to learn that people tend to do better when they know better. When we educate our employees and volunteers about discrimination and harassment, we will come to learn that these individuals are better equipped to make the right decision whenever the opportunity arises.

Wage and Hour Compliance

Religious non-profit organizations, while driven by a sense of mission and purpose, must navigate legal obligations to ensure fair treatment of their employees. Neglecting wage and hour compliance, as stipulated by the Fair Labor Standards Act (FLSA), can have significant legal implications. It is imperative for these churches to meticulously adhere to minimum wage and overtime pay requirements, recognizing that failure to do so may lead to legal repercussions.

Additionally, the proper classification of employees as exempt or non-exempt is crucial, as misclassifications can also result in violations of the FLSA. Ensuring compliance with wage and hour regulations demonstrates the willingness of these communities of faith to uphold principles of fairness and justice.

Occupational Safety and Health Administration (OSHA) Compliance

Neglecting to provide a safe and healthy workplace, as mandated by OSHA regulations, can expose churches to significant legal implications. It is essential for them to prioritize adherence to safety standards, ensuring that their facilities and practices meet OSHA requirements.

Additionally, prompt reporting of workplace injuries is crucial to maintain transparency and compliance. By diligently addressing OSHA regulations, religious non-profit organizations not only fulfill their legal obligations but also create an environment where employees, volunteers, and beneficiaries can engage in their mission with confidence, knowing that their well-being is prioritized and protected.

Privacy and Confidentiality

Failing to safeguard employee privacy, particularly concerning sensitive information such as medical records, can lead to severe legal consequences. It is imperative for these organizations to adhere to data protection laws that govern the collection, storage, and usage of personal information. Ensuring the confidentiality of employee data not only upholds ethical standards but also mitigates the risk of legal challenges. By prioritizing privacy measures, religious non-profit organizations not only demonstrate respect for the individuals they serve and employ, they also establish trust and foster a secure and harmonious environment within their communities.

Employment Eligibility Verification (Form I-9)

The Form I-9, officially known as the Employment Eligibility Verification, is a mandatory U.S. government form used by employers to verify an employee's identity and their authorization to legally work in the United States. All U.S. employers must ensure proper completion of Form I-9 for everyone they hire for employment in the United States, including both citizens and noncitizens. Every employee hired after November 6, 1986, must complete an I-9 Form at the time of hire. The employee must complete Section 1 of the form no later than the first day of employment. The employer, or an authorized representative of the employer, must complete Section 2 within three business days of the employee's first day of employment.

Neglecting to verify the identity and employment eligibility of all employees or maintain accurate and up-to-date records can result in severe legal consequences. Compliance with these regulations is not only a legal obligation but also a commitment to fairness and integrity in employment practices. By rigorously following the guidelines outlined in Form I-9, religious non-profit organizations not only fulfill their legal responsibilities but also contribute to a transparent and lawful employment environment, ultimately preserving the trust and credibility essential to their mission-driven work.

Workers' Compensation

Worker's compensation insurance is a type of insurance that provides benefits to employees who sustained on-the-job injury or illness. The specific purpose of this insurance is to cover medical expenses, rehabilitation costs and lost wages for these injured employees. It provides a layer of protection for both the employee as well as the employer. In the case of the employees, it provides financial support and medical care, regardless of who is at fault. For the employer, they can fulfill their legal obligation of providing compensation (income replacement) for work-related injuries, while also providing them with immunity from lawsuits resulting from workplace injuries.

Because the specific benefits and requirements of workers' compensation insurance can vary depending on the state or country where the employer operates, it is important for those who are responsible take time out to study the specific requirements within their respective jurisdiction and ensure compliance.

Employee Benefits Compliance

Comply with federal and state laws related to employee benefits, including health insurance and retirement plans. Ensuring compliance with employee benefits regulations is critical. In the United States, group health insurance is a mandatory benefit that employers with fifty or more full-time employees must offer under the Affordable Care Act (ACA). Non-compliance can result in hefty fines. In addition to health insurance, employers are also required to offer long-term disability insurance to provide income to eligible employees who become disabled and are unable to work for an extended period. Paid leave requirements vary depending on state and local laws, but all employers must comply with the federal Family and Medical Leave Act (FMLA), which requires eligible employees to receive up to twelve weeks of unpaid leave for specified family and medical reasons. Employers who fail to comply with these regulations risk facing legal action from employees and government agencies, and even being "tried in the court of public opinion," which can tarnish an organization's reputation. Therefore, employers must stay informed about changes in employee benefits regulations and proactively ensure their compliance to avoid any legal issues.

Anti-Retaliation Policies

Develop and enforce policies prohibiting retaliation against employees who assert their rights under employment laws.

In addition to the development of policies prohibiting retaliation, we should also encourage reporting of workplace violations without fear of reprisal.

Sexual Harassment Prevention and Reporting

Sexual harassment in any workplace, including a church setting, is a serious issue that undermines the safety, trust, and integrity of the work environment. It's crucial to recognize that even within religious organizations devoted to spiritual service and moral guidance, sexual harassment can occur, and it needs to be addressed with as much urgency and seriousness as in any other workplace.

Sexual harassment is defined as unwanted and unwelcome behavior of a sexual nature that may include unwanted sexual advances, requests for sexual favors, verbal or nonverbal communications of a sexual nature, and physical conduct of a sexual nature. Harassment creates a hostile, intimidating, or offensive work environment and can take the form of quid pro quo harassment or create a hostile work environment. In a church setting, victims of sexual harassment could be employees, volunteers, congregation members, or any individuals associated with church activities.

Churches must implement policies to prevent and respond to sexual harassment. Prevention starts with clear guidelines and anti-harassment training for all employees and leaders. A safe and accessible reporting mechanism should be established, guaranteeing confidentiality and protection from retaliation.

A prompt, effective, and impartial investigation should follow any reports. Consequences for perpetrators should be consistent and significant enough to deter future incidents and affirm the church's commitment to a safe work environment.

Recordkeeping Requirements

Churches have a duty to maintain accurate and complete employment records as required by federal and state law. If there are headquarters that provide a centralized system of management for your church, it is best that this aspect of the record-keeping takes place at that location. Otherwise, this is a role that should be handled by a human resource practitioner or office administrator.

Maintain records related to hiring, promotions, terminations, and other employment actions. Disciplinary actions can also be retained but are recommended to only be accessible by a select few, preferably those who are in human resources.

Unemployment Insurance Compliance

Where applicable, churches are to comply with state unemployment insurance requirements. Efforts should also be made to respond to unemployment claims promptly and accurately.

Nonprofit Tax Exemption Compliance

Comply with IRS regulations to maintain tax-exempt status. Ensure proper financial transparency and reporting. The scope and gravity of this cannot be overstated. It is important that churches consult and retain the services of a certified public accountant (CPA) on how they may remain compliant with IRS regulations and tax codes.

CHAPTER 20

Insurance Coverages Required for Employees

Churches and religious organizations simply cannot take on all the risks associated with their operations. Adequate insurance coverage plays a pivotal role in providing a safety net for unforeseen circumstances, ranging from health crises to workplace injuries, thus fostering an environment where employees can focus on their roles with peace of mind.

There are a number of key insurance coverages that faith-based entities should have in place.

1. Health Insurance (Medical, Pharmacy & Dental): Provide comprehensive health insurance coverage for employees to address medical expenses, prescriptions, and preventive care. Explore options for group health plans to make coverage more accessible and cost-effective.

2. Workers' Compensation: Obtain workers' compensation insurance to provide financial protection for employees in the event of work-related injuries or illnesses. This coverage is set up to help employees receive financial indemnification for job-related injuries. In some cases where the employee is unable to return to work, it serves as income replacement, and will also cover medical expenses incurred because of the injury. Comply with state workers' compensation coverage regulations to ensure legal compliance and support injured workers.

3. Group Life Insurance: Offer life insurance coverage to employees, which provides financial security to their families in the event of an employee's untimely death. Consider group life insurance policies that can be more affordable and easier to administer.

4. Disability Insurance: Provide disability insurance to protect employees' income in the event of a disabling illness or injury. Consider both short-term and long-term disability coverage to address varying needs.

5. Liability Insurance: Secure general liability insurance to protect against claims of bodily injury or property damage arising from the organization's operations. Consider professional liability insurance to cover claims related to professional advice or services provided by the organization. This is particularly important for churches that provide counseling services to the community. Some counselors have their own.

6. Employment Practices Liability: Obtain EPLI coverage to protect against claims related to employment practices, such as discrimination, wrongful termination, or harassment. EPLI may cover legal defense costs, settlements, and judgments.

7. Directors, Officers, and Trustees Liability: Provide DO&T insurance to protect the personal assets of board members and leaders in the event of lawsuits alleging wrongful acts in management decisions. Having DO&T insurance can make it easier to attract and retain qualified individuals to serve on the board. Recently, I have learned that many DO&T Liability coverages do not carry coverage for discrimination allegations brought against the organization by non-employees. In this case, there should be a third-party rider that is purchased specifically to address these claims.

8. Cyber Liability Insurance: In an increasingly digital world, consider cyber liability insurance to protect against the financial consequences of data breaches, cyberattacks, or privacy violations.

9. Volunteer Labor Insurance: In the absence of workers compensation coverage, many volunteers have been forced to seek legal remedies for injuries sustained while engaging in church projects and activities. Volunteer labor insurance is one way that churches may safeguard against this, by purchasing coverage for their volunteers.

CHAPTER 21

Supplemental Insurance Coverages

Supplemental accident insurance for camps, sports, and trips can greatly benefit a church by providing additional coverage beyond what may be offered by primary insurance policies or by filling gaps in coverage where primary insurance falls short. Here are detailed descriptions of how this type of insurance can benefit a church.

Enhanced Protection: Supplemental accident insurance enhances the level of protection for participants involved in church-sponsored activities such as camps, sports programs, and trips. It serves as a safety net, ensuring that individuals are covered in the event of accidents, injuries, or medical emergencies that may occur during these activities.

Comprehensive Coverage: This type of insurance typically offers comprehensive coverage for a wide range of accidents and injuries, including medical expenses, emergency treatment, hospitalization, ambulance services, and follow-up care. It may also include coverage for accidental death and dismemberment, providing financial support to the individual or their family in the event of a tragic outcome.

Supplementary Benefits: In addition to covering medical expenses directly related to accidents or injuries, supplemental accident insurance may offer supplementary benefits such as coverage for rehabilitation services, physical therapy, prosthetics, and transportation expenses incurred as a result of the injury. These additional benefits can help alleviate the financial burden on the injured individual and their family during the recovery process.

No-fault Coverage: Supplemental accident insurance typically provides no-fault coverage, meaning that benefits are paid regardless of who is at fault for the accident or injury. This can be particularly beneficial in situations where liability may be difficult to determine, such as during sports activities or recreational outings.

Affordable Premiums: Supplemental accident insurance policies often come with affordable premiums, making them a cost-effective way for churches to provide additional protection for participants in camps, sports programs, and trips. By investing in this type of insurance, churches can demonstrate their commitment to the safety and well-being of their members and participants without breaking the bank.

Peace of Mind: Perhaps most importantly, supplemental accident insurance provides peace of mind to both the church and its participants. Knowing that individuals are covered in the event of an accident or injury can alleviate concerns and allow everyone involved to fully enjoy the activities and experiences being offered by the church. This sense of security can strengthen the trust and confidence that members and participants have in the church leadership and its commitment to their welfare.

Overall, supplemental accident insurance for camps, sports, and trips is a valuable risk management tool for churches that offers enhanced protection, comprehensive coverage, and peace of mind for both the church and its participants. By investing in this type of insurance, churches can ensure that they are prepared to respond effectively to accidents and injuries that may occur during their activities, while also demonstrating their commitment to the safety and well-being of their members and participants.

CHAPTER 22

Volunteer Management

Without the help, participation, and commitment of volunteers, the doors of many churches would remain closed. Given the heavy reliance on volunteer work, churches must give very special attention to the way they choose to manage their volunteers.

Effective management of volunteers can help churches achieve their mission and objectives. However, it takes a lot of planning, coordination, and effort to maximize this crucial aspect of your ministry. In this section, we will explore some of the best practices for managing volunteers that can be implemented by churches of all sizes.

Recruitment: To find the right volunteers for the task, the recruitment process must be tailored to the specific needs of the church. Create a job description for each available position to clearly specify the expectations and responsibilities of the volunteer. Use digital platforms such as social media, church websites, and email lists to advertise volunteer opportunities, and don't forget to leverage word-of-mouth by actively engaging with the church congregation.

Training: Before a volunteer begins their work, they need to have the necessary skills and knowledge to perform their role effectively. Be sure to provide comprehensive training that outlines the duties, expectations, and performance standards for each position. Consider pairing new recruits with veteran volunteers to facilitate learning through observation and practice.

Communication: Clear and consistent communication is essential for volunteer management. Establish a channel for communication and ensure that volunteers are kept informed about church activities, schedules, and any other pertinent information. In addition, offer feedback and recognition to volunteers to maintain morale and motivation.

Evaluation: Churches must regularly evaluate volunteer performance to ensure that they are fulfilling their responsibilities and meeting the desired outcomes. Consider creating feedback mechanisms such as surveys, questionnaires, or focus groups to gather data that can be used to improve the performance of the volunteers and the effectiveness of the volunteer program overall.

Appreciation: Volunteers deserve to be recognized and appreciated for their hard work and dedication. Celebrate their contributions through events or ceremonies that highlight their achievements. Offering small tokens such as thank-you notes, gift cards, or other forms of recognition can go a long way in showing appreciation for their time and effort.

By incorporating these best practices for volunteer management, churches can build a culture of volunteerism and ensure that they are utilizing their resources effectively to achieve their mission and goals. Taking the time to manage volunteers well will pay off in dividends as the church grows and the impact of volunteer efforts becomes widespread.

In one of their recent publications on volunteer management, Church Mutual Insurance company published three very sad cases of volunteers who were injured while serving at churches. In the first case, a volunteer who was painting from a scaffolding suffered a severe fall, resulting in a head injury and subsequent coma.

Another volunteer faced extensive injuries and weeks of lost income after falling from a ladder while assisting with a building project. And finally, an aspiring young pianist, volunteering in a ministry's remodeling project, experienced a tragic accident where several fingers were severed by a table saw.

All three of these cases are very sad tales of what can happen in the absence of sound risk management practices. The services provided by volunteers are invaluable, but when they are not managed appropriately, they can also pose as one of the church's greatest liabilities. Volunteers face similar injuries as regular employees and may also inadvertently cause harm for which the organization becomes legally responsible. Following are some ways in which the legal exposure related to volunteers is amplified.

1. Limited Legal Protection: In many states, volunteer workers are not covered by workers' compensation laws. This means that employers are not shielded by the immunity present in workers compensation laws. And volunteers, unlike paid employees, must navigate the civil justice system to seek compensation for serious injuries sustained during their volunteer activities.

2. The Number of Hours Worked: The sheer number of volunteer workers and the total hours they contribute often surpass those of paid employees. This increased scale magnifies the potential risks and liabilities associated with volunteer engagement.

3. Training and Skill Disparities: Volunteer workers frequently possess less training, fewer skills, and inadequate equipment for the diverse range of duties they undertake. This lack of preparation can contribute to increased risk during their service.

Section III: Protecting Property

CHAPTER 23

Securing Sacred Spaces: Facilities Management for Houses of Worship

The physical infrastructure that houses and facilitates ministry activities plays a crucial role in the overall success of any community of faith. Members look forward to meeting up in these physical spaces on a weekly basis, and sometimes multiple times per week, to connect with their fellow members, worship and engage in community outreach activities. This is why it is crucial that church leaders take a very intentional approach when determining the best course of action to protect the physical and financial assets of the church. Neglecting this fundamental aspect of ministry can exert a profoundly detrimental impact on the church's capacity to effectively fulfill its mission.

In this section, we take a deep dive into the diverse strategies that can be implemented by your church to ensure the protection of the tangible and intangible assets for the church, ranging from finances to property and equipment.

The landscape of property insurance has shifted significantly; churches are forced to pay higher premiums for less coverage. To maintain an A+ rating with reinsurers, and to improve their overall profitability, insurance companies are now imposing higher deductibles for the most common perils that affect covered properties. In navigating this evolving terrain, it becomes imperative for church leadership to be astute risk managers, cognizant of the heightened financial burdens accompanying property-related exposures.

The effective management of financial resources demands a paradigm shift, particularly in the way we perceive preventative maintenance and repairs. Rather than viewing these activities as mere expenses, leaders must recognize them as strategic investments in the longevity and resilience of their ministry. This shift in perspective is essential for establishing a harmonious equilibrium between accomplishing the mission and fortifying the physical structures against the diverse risks they may encounter. So, what does that look like in a practical sense?

CHURCH RISK MANAGEMENT PROCESS

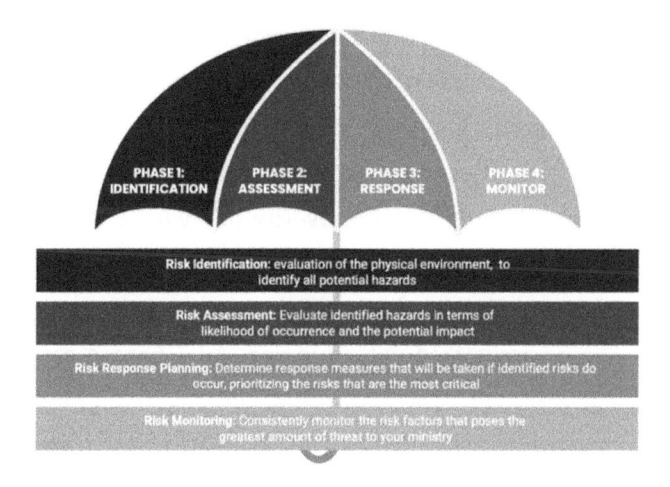

PHASE 1: IDENTIFICATION
PHASE 2: ASSESSMENT
PHASE 3: RESPONSE
PHASE 4: MONITOR

Risk Identification: evaluation of the physical environment, to identify all potential hazards

Risk Assessment: Evaluate identified hazards in terms of likelihood of occurrence and the potential impact

Risk Response Planning: Determine response measures that will be taken if identified risks do occur, prioritizing the risks that are the most critical

Risk Monitoring: Consistently monitor the risk factors that poses the greatest amount of threat to your ministry

1. The process begins with a physical walk-through, a meticulous examination of the physical environment, encompassing the church building, surrounding property, and installed assets. Identifying and categorizing potential hazards, from natural disasters to security vulnerabilities, is paramount to this assessment. For example, if during the walkthrough a crack in the walkway of the church is identified, this should be listed on the sheet.

2. The next step is to conduct rigorous analysis of the identified risk in terms of the likelihood that it will occur and the severity of its impact if it should take place, allowing for the allocation and prioritization of resources to assist with mitigation strategies. Using the example of the cracked walkway identified

in item one above, in this next step the assessment could then assign a score of between 0-10 in terms of the likelihood that a personal injury accident could possibly occur. Given the fact many people wear heels to church, this issue could result in sprained ankles or, in a worst-case scenario, broken bones. If this should take place the severity of such a risk would likely rank higher. So if the likelihood of occurrence is determined to be 8 and the severity is 10, the risk score associated with this particular hazard can be determined. The risk score would then be eight multiplied by 10 divided by two (8x10=80/2) which would be 40. With a risk score of 40, given the fact that the highest possible risk score is 50, this risk would be ranked as high on the list of priorities.

3. Church leadership must then formulate and implement risk mitigation plans, incorporating preventative measures, emergency response protocols, and asset protection strategies. Regular reviews and updates of these plans to ensure adaptability to evolving circumstances, fostering a dynamic risk management framework attuned to the unique challenges inherent in the physical church setting. Continuing our working example of the cracked walkway, a risk that high should be resolved as soon as possible. So when this information is shared wth the board, it becomes easier for decisions to be made and for response action to be taken.

Through this methodical process, the church not only safeguards its tangible assets but also cultivates resilience in the face of unforeseen events, thereby upholding its mission with steadfastness and preparedness.

Risk Assessment for Churches: Church Self-Inspection Survey

Church self-inspection surveys provide an essential and valuable opportunity for these organizations to assess and identify potential hazards that may pose a threat to members, property, and operations. Conducting annual surveys can help churches plan and prioritize resources that will address areas of concern and enhance the safety and security of their premises.

Annual self-inspection surveys enable churches to identify structural, electrical, and environmental hazards that can lead to accidents, injuries, and property damage. These surveys are tools that churches use to identify potential fire hazards, such as overloaded electrical outlets and improperly stored flammable materials. Additionally, the surveys can help identify structural deficiencies such as missing handrails or steps, uneven or slippery flooring, and unsafe outdoor walking surfaces. It is particularly helpful in identifying the things that an untrained eye would miss.

The process of conducting a self-inspection survey also provides an opportunity for the church to review their emergency response procedures and make necessary updates. A comprehensive emergency response plan can help minimize the impact of any disaster and ensure that church members and employees are in a stronger position to respond to catastrophic events.

In Allegheny East Conference, we perform one self-inspection per year. The information gleaned from the survey helps us to gather much needed insights on the state of affairs within our churches. To increase the rate of participation, we make a big deal each year about the completion of the self-inspection survey, by incentivizing the program. At our trainings, we emphasize the need for safety officers to use the deficiencies and gaps identified in the survey as the basis for which they recommend action items and projects to the church board as part of their reports.

The majority of insurance carriers provide this free resource to their clients to help them with the risk assessment process. You may also make use of the free tool available on the *protectingthesacred.org* website.

CHAPTER 24

Responding to Property Risks: Common Risks Associated with Church Properties

Common Risks Associated with Church Properties

Churches that engage in risk identification should view this process as a proactive approach to safeguarding the well-being of congregations and preserving the sanctity of these spaces. We will now identify risks, then analyze and apply the risk response planning process. By addressing these risks systematically and implementing preventive measures, church leaders can create a secure environment that fosters spiritual growth and community engagement. In this book, we've done some of the heavy lifting for you. Following are some of the most common risks that affect the physical and financial assets within churches. We will share some of the actionable steps that may be taken in order to mitigate, prevent, or respond to these risk factors.

Natural Disasters

Churches are susceptible to a range of natural disasters, including earthquakes, floods, hurricanes, tornadoes, and wildfires. Identifying the geographical location and associated risks is crucial to your ministry. Conducting a comprehensive risk assessment, consulting with local emergency management authorities, and implementing structural reinforcements can help minimize the impact of natural disasters. Please see below important information on the most common natural disasters that churches face:

Responding to Earthquakes

Some regions tend to be far more susceptible to earthquakes than others. If you live in an area where earthquakes are a common occurrence, it is highly recommended that you engage the services of structural engineers to identify the sections of your building that would be most vulnerable to such an event. These are also referred to as seismic risk assessments. Based on the seismic risk assessment conducted, consider implementing structural retrofits to enhance the building's resilience to earthquakes. These may include reinforcing walls, adding bracing, or installing base isolators to minimize the impact of ground shaking.

While we are primarily addressing how you may fortify your physical plant against such an event, please see section II on how you may prepare your congregation for an event that might occur while worship is in session. There are many insurance carriers that list earth movement as a named exclusion on their policies. It is important that you speak with your carrier to learn more about your coverages in this regard and plan accordingly. Depending on your location, you may be able to purchase a separate rider specific for earthquakes.

Floods

Responding to floods requires a proactive risk management approach to safeguard both the congregation and the church property. Here are essential steps that churches can take to mitigate flood risks and respond effectively:

1. Conduct a Flood Risk Assessment: Start by assessing the flood risk of the church property. Determine if the church is located in a flood-prone area and evaluate the potential severity of flooding. Consult with local authorities, meteorological services, and floodplain management agencies for up-to-date information.

2. Implement Flood-resistant Building Design: If possible, consider implementing flood-resistant building designs or retrofits. Elevate electrical systems and utilities above potential flood levels, install flood barriers, and use water-resistant building materials to minimize damage in the event of a flood.

3. Establish Emergency Procedures: Develop and communicate clear emergency procedures for floods. Educate congregants, staff, and volunteers on evacuation routes, assembly points, and emergency contacts. Regularly conduct drills to ensure that everyone is familiar with the procedures.

4. Create Flood Emergency Kits: Stock emergency kits with essentials such as first aid supplies, flashlights, batteries, non-perishable food, water, and blankets. Ensure that these kits are easily accessible and periodically check and refresh the supplies.

5. Install Flood Monitoring Systems: Utilize flood monitoring systems to receive early warnings of potential flooding. These systems can provide valuable time for the church community to take preventive measures or evacuate. Stay informed about weather forecasts and flood alerts from local authorities.

6. Secure Important Documents: Safeguard important documents such as insurance policies, financial records, and other critical paperwork by storing them in waterproof containers. Consider maintaining digital backups of essential documents in a secure off-site location.

7. Elevate Equipment and Furnishings: Elevate electrical equipment, appliances, and furnishings above potential flood levels. This includes audio-visual equipment, sound systems, and any valuable religious artifacts. Consider using raised platforms or shelving to keep these items out of harm's way.

8. Collaborate with Local Authorities: Establish a relationship with local emergency management agencies, fire departments, and other relevant authorities. Understand local flood evacuation plans and coordinate with these entities to enhance the effectiveness of emergency response efforts.

9. Review and Update Insurance Coverage: Many of the property insurance coverages that exist for churches do not automatically cover floods. As a matter of fact, if you live in a flood zone, many churches are required to purchase flood insurance as a separate rider. It is important that members of the church's leadership team evaluate (based on their location) if they are in such a region and purchase the coverage as needed. If you do have coverage, consult with your flood insurance carriers to ensure that the policy adequately covers the church property and its contents.

10. Educate the Congregation: Educate the congregation about flood preparedness and the importance of individual responsibility. Provide information on how to secure homes and personal belongings in the event of flooding and encourage congregants to have their own emergency plans in place.

11. Implement Landscaping Strategies: Work with landscaping professionals to implement strategies that promote water drainage away from the building. This may include grading the land, installing drainage systems, and using permeable surfaces to reduce the risk of flooding.

By taking these steps, churches can enhance their resilience to floods and protect both the physical infrastructure and the well-being of the congregation. Regular training, drills, and collaboration with local authorities are key components of a comprehensive flood risk management strategy.

Preventing and Responding to Wild and Electrical Fires

Wildfires are catastrophic disasters that have been on the rise in recent years. The damage caused by these fires has been monumental, with entire towns and ecosystems being destroyed in a matter of hours. The cost of such damage has also been staggering, with billions of dollars in losses incurred over the years.

According to the Cybersecurity and Infrastructure Security Agency (CISA), within the United States alone, the 2020 wildfire season was the worst in history, with a record-breaking 8.3 million acres burned.[1] The total cost of the damages in California alone is estimated to be around $10 billion. This staggering number doesn't only include the immediate costs of fighting the fire, but also the long-term impact on the local economy, such as the loss of homes, businesses, and job opportunities. Numerous churches and Christian schools were impacted by these fires. While the causes of these fires are primarily from lightning, there are some fires due to human action. Regardless of the cause, here are some things that you can do to protect your facilities or to mitigate the risks associated with wildfires:

1. Create Defensible Space: Work with local fire authorities to establish a defensible space around the church property. This involves reducing vegetation, clearing debris, and creating a buffer zone to help prevent the spread of wildfires.

2. Firebreaks and Barriers: Implement firebreaks and barriers using non-combustible materials to hinder the progress of wildfires. These barriers can be strategically placed to protect the church buildings and surrounding areas.

3. Regular Vegetation Maintenance: Schedule regular maintenance to control vegetation growth on and around the property. Prune trees and bushes, remove dead vegetation, and create a landscape that is less susceptible to rapid fire spread.

4. Emergency Water Sources: Ensure there are emergency water sources on the property. This may include installing fire hydrants, maintaining water tanks, or having access to nearby water sources that can be utilized by firefighting teams.

5. Evacuation Planning: Develop and communicate evacuation plans in case of a wildfire threat. Clearly define evacuation routes, assembly points, and procedures for ensuring the safe exit of congregants, staff, and volunteers.

6. Collaboration with Emergency Services: Establish a partnership with local firefighting agencies. Work with them to understand the local wildfire risk, receive early warnings, and coordinate response efforts. Regularly participate in community drills to enhance preparedness.

Electrical Fire Prevention:

1. Regular Electrical Inspections: Conduct regular inspections of the church's electrical systems. Engage qualified electricians to identify and address potential hazards, faulty wiring, or outdated components that may pose a risk of electrical fires. The frequency of these inspections should be determined based on the age of the building.

2. Install Fire Detection Systems: Install fire detection and alarm systems throughout the church buildings. Ensure that these systems are regularly tested and well-maintained. Early detection is critical for preventing the escalation of electrical fires.

3. Implement Electrical Safety Policies: Develop and enforce electrical safety policies. Train staff and volunteers on safe practices, including the proper use of electrical equipment, avoiding overloading circuits, and promptly reporting any electrical issues.

4. Regular Equipment Maintenance: Regularly maintain and service electrical equipment, including heating systems, appliances, and lighting fixtures. Overheating and malfunctioning equipment are common causes of electrical fires.

5. Emergency Response Training: Provide training for staff and volunteers on how to respond to electrical fires. This includes using fire extinguishers, initiating emergency shutdown procedures, and evacuating the premises safely.

6. Install Automatic Fire Suppression Systems: Consider installing automatic fire suppression systems, such as sprinklers, in areas with a high risk of electrical fires. These systems can help contain and extinguish a fire before it spreads.

7. Emergency Power Shutoff Procedures: Establish procedures for safely shutting off power in case of an electrical fire. Clearly mark electrical panels, train designated personnel to perform shutdowns, and communicate these procedures to all relevant parties.

8. Emergency Contact Information: Maintain an updated list of emergency contacts, including local fire departments and utility providers. This information should be readily available to expedite communication and coordination in case of an emergency.

Preventing and Responding to Wind-related Damage

Losses related to wind are on the rise—hurricanes, tornadoes, and severe windstorms. Many insurance carriers have been forced to take extraordinary steps to limit the financial impact this event can have on them as insurance companies, and as such, this has left churches in a very vulnerable financial state. Because of this financial strain, the number-one response measure that churches can use to combat this threat is to get on the offensive by fortifying their roofs and adopting measures that are preventative in nature. Here are some steps that may be taken to reduce the impact or prevent such weather conditions from damaging your buildings excessively in the event of wind or hail damage.

1. Strong and Durable Roofing Material: Churches should invest in strong and durable roofing materials such as metal roofing or asphalt shingles that can withstand strong wind gusts and heavy hailstones. These materials are less likely to be affected by high winds and hail damage. A strong and durable roof can play a crucial role in protecting the church interior from water damage.

2. Regular Roof Inspections: Churches must have their roofs inspected regularly to identify any potential damage or areas that require maintenance. Regular roof inspections reveal weak points that can be easily addressed before they become major problems. It is essential to take preventative measures before severe weather strikes to prevent damage or leaks that could cause considerable damage.

3. Proper Tree Maintenance: Trees are beautiful, and they add a lovely aesthetic to any church landscape. However, if they are not properly maintained, they can become a grave hazard during severe windstorms. Church property owners should ensure that trees are trimmed regularly and pruned to prevent branches from falling onto the structure of the building. This preventative step reduces the risk of any injury to church members and minimizes the impact of severe winds.

4. Reinforce Doors and Windows: Doors and windows are usually the weakest points in any building, and they are most prone to damage during high winds. Churches should invest in storm shutters or impact-resistant glass to protect the windows from flying debris. Installing hurricane-rated doors or door tracks and sealing them with caulk or weather stripping can prevent water damage during heavy rainfall.

5. *Plan for Evacuation:* As a final measure, churches must have an evacuation plan in place in case of severe weather emergencies. This plan should include procedures for evacuation, sheltering-in-place, and communication procedures, including designated safe areas in the building.

Churches can take several measures to reduce the impact of wind and hail damage. Investing in strong roofing materials, regular roof inspections, tree maintenance, reinforcing doors and windows, and having an emergency plan in place will minimize damage, protect church members and property, and ensure the longevity of the building structure.

Preventing Water Damage from Frozen Pipes in Church Buildings

Water damage caused by frozen pipes is a common and often costly issue during the winter months. In a church setting, where the preservation of the building is not only essential for the congregation but also carries significant sentimental value, it is crucial to implement proactive measures to mitigate the risk of frozen pipes and subsequent water damage. This section discusses key strategies for effective risk management in preventing frozen pipes in church buildings.

1. Temperature and Flood Sensors: Installing temperature and flood sensors throughout the church premises is an integral part of an advanced risk management system. These sensors can detect drops in temperature and alert facility managers or designated personnel when temperatures approach levels that could lead to frozen pipes. Flood sensors are equally important, as they can quickly identify water leaks and potential pipe bursts, allowing for swift response to prevent extensive damage.

2. Winterized Buildings: Winterizing the church building is a fundamental step in preventing frozen pipes. This involves a comprehensive inspection of the building's infrastructure to identify vulnerable areas and taking necessary precautions. Some key winterization steps include:

- a. Insulating exposed pipes: Ensure that pipes in attics, basements, and crawl spaces are properly insulated to prevent exposure to freezing temperatures.
- b. Sealing gaps and cracks: Identify and seal any gaps or cracks in the building's exterior that could allow cold air to infiltrate and affect interior temperatures.
- c. Weatherstripping doors and windows: Properly sealing doors and windows with weatherstripping can significantly reduce drafts and help maintain a warmer indoor environment.

3. Increase Building Temperature: Maintaining a consistent and adequate indoor temperature is essential in preventing frozen pipes. During colder months, consider adjusting the thermostat to keep the building temperature above the freezing point. This measure is especially important for areas with a higher risk of frozen pipes, such as those located near exterior walls or in unheated spaces.

4. Drain the Pipes Throughout the Building: An effective strategy to prevent frozen pipes is to drain water from the plumbing system when the building is not in use or during extended periods of extreme cold. This can be achieved by

a. Draining outdoor faucets and sprinkler systems.
b. Emptying water from unused bathrooms or areas of the church.
c. Running a small, steady stream of water through faucets to keep water moving and prevent freezing.

By implementing a proactive plan that includes the use of temperature and flood sensors, winterization measures, maintaining a consistent building temperature, and draining pipes, churches can significantly reduce the risk of water damage from frozen pipes. This proactive approach not only safeguards the structural integrity of the building but also ensures a safe and welcoming environment for the congregation.

CHAPTER 25

Burglary and Theft Prevention

In times past, bad actors refrained from stealing from churches in fear of the perceived retribution they would receive because of stealing from God. Those days are long gone. From burglary and theft to acts of violence and terrorism, churches are vulnerable to a multitude of security risks that can have severe consequences. While churches may not be able to fully prevent all these incidents, it is wise and responsible stewardship to implement certain safeguards that will either prevent or reduce the impact they will have on the overall operations of the church.

Burglary and Theft

Burglary and theft are serious concerns for many churches, especially when valuable items like copper and high-end multimedia electronics are at risk. Fortunately, there are several steps that churches can take to prevent and reduce the impact of these crimes.

1. Install Security Cameras: The first step to prevent burglary and theft is to install a quality security camera system that can monitor all parts of the church. Having visible cameras sends a message to would-be thieves that the church takes security seriously.

2. Use Technology to Your Advantage: Modern security systems often come equipped with motion detectors, sirens, and other security features to alert church authorities of any breaches. Some systems also have remote access and monitoring via a smartphone app to monitor the church from anywhere.

3. Add Lighting: An additional deterrent to prevent theft is the installation of lighting around vulnerable areas of the church, such as windows, doors, and parking lots. Motion-activated lights that illuminate when movement is detected can also draw attention to the area and deter burglars.

4. Secure Doors and Windows: Churches should ensure all doors and windows are secure and have quality locks to prevent forced entry. Installing steel doors or metal security gates can further enhance security.

5. Keep Valuables out of Sight: Ensure that valuable items like copper and electronics are kept out of sight and locked away to prevent theft. Consider storing valuables in a safe or secure cabinet, or using burglar bars for equipment that must be stored outdoors such as AC units or compressors.

6. Hire a Security Guard: Churches can consider hiring a security guard or contracting with a security firm to provide round-the-clock surveillance and protection. This would mainly apply to larger churches with the budget to afford such services.

7. Educate Congregation and Staff: Educate the congregation and staff about the importance of security and encourage them to report any suspicious activity. Establishing a culture of security awareness can go a long way in preventing theft and burglary.

Preventing and reducing the impact of burglary and theft in churches requires a multi-faceted approach. Churches should focus on securing the building, installing security cameras, reinforcing doors and windows, adding lighting, securing valuables, and hiring a security guard. A vigilant congregation and staff who are aware of security issues can also play an essential role in preventing theft and thwarting crime. Implementing these steps can help churches protect themselves and ensure the safety and protection of their congregation.

Vandalism

When Pastor Mitchell received a phone call that there had been shots fired at his church, he immediately sprang into action. The police were contacted, while he along with several of the other church deacons made their way to the facility. It was strange, because at the time it happened, there was no scheduled activity at the church. While he wasn't worried that anyone had been harmed, the incident was still alarming. *Why would anyone fire gunshots at my church?* was a lingering question on his mind. As he approached the church, the police were already on the scene. Some of the neighbors had called in the incident as well.

Thankfully, as he suspected, no one was hurt. Several of the windows were shattered, and sections of the roof and guttering were damaged by bullets. The whole thing was captured on their surveillance camera.

During their investigation, law enforcement shared with the pastor that the angry soon-to-be ex-husband of one of his prominent members took his frustration out on the church where his soon-to-be ex-wife was very well regarded. An arrest was made, and the church worked with law enforcement and the insurance company to resolve the matter. The video surveillance was quite helpful in solving this case.

Churches are often targets for vandalism due to other factors such as their historical, cultural, and religious value. The damage caused by such incidents can have a severe emotional and financial impact on congregations. Here are some of the recommended steps that can be taken to prevent or respond to vandalism at your church.

Enhancing Security Measures for Churches

1. Install Security Cameras: Installing security cameras is a fundamental step in deterring vandalism on church premises. Visible camera systems act as a deterrent, making vandals think twice before committing acts of destruction. Furthermore, cameras provide valuable evidence in case of an incident. The placement, quality and signage for security cameras are crucial elements in completing this important step.

- **Placement:** When installing the cameras, consider placing cameras strategically to cover key entry points, parking lots, and vulnerable areas.
- **Quality:** Not all security cameras are created equal. Good image quality goes a long way in helping security teams identify perpetrators of crimes. Be very meticulous and selective about the brand of cameras you choose to invest in. Additionally, when purchasing security cameras, it is always best to opt for high-resolution cameras with night vision capabilities for optimal surveillance, even in low-light conditions. There are some great brands available. While we do not endorse any specific brands, we urge members of the church security team to take these factors into consideration.
- **Signage:** Ensure proper signage indicating the presence of surveillance cameras to reinforce their deterrent effect.

2. Install Security Lighting: Well-lit surroundings discourage vandals, as they are less likely to engage in illegal activities under bright lights. Motion sensor lights are particularly effective in detecting movement and alerting authorities or security personnel whenever suspicious activities are taking place around your building. To achieve the best results, it is important that they:

- Install lighting fixtures with motion sensors around the church perimeter and parking lot.
- Regularly maintain lighting systems to ensure they remain functional and effective.
- Consider installing timer-controlled lights to illuminate the church exterior during nighttime hours.

3. Create a Community Watch Program: Engaging with the local community and establishing a community watch program can significantly enhance security efforts. This program encourages residents to be vigilant and report any suspicious activity around the church promptly.

- Host community meetings to discuss the importance of vigilance and encourage participation in the watch program.
- Provide training or informational sessions on identifying and reporting suspicious behavior.
- Establish communication channels, such as a dedicated hotline or email address, for community members to report concerns or incidents.

4. Implement a Key Control System: Preventing unauthorized entry is essential for maintaining security. Implementing a key control system ensures that access to church facilities is limited to authorized individuals, such as employees and volunteers.

- Keep a record of keys issued and maintain strict protocols for key distribution and retrieval.
- Consider upgrading to electronic access control systems for enhanced security and accountability.
- Regularly review and update access privileges to align with staffing changes or organizational needs.

5. Build Perimeter Walls or Fences: Physical barriers, such as perimeter walls or fences, create a deterrent against vandalism by restricting access to the church premises.

- Choose durable materials and ensure proper installation to maximize effectiveness.
- Incorporate landscaping elements, such as thorny shrubs or hedges, as additional deterrents along the perimeter.
- Regularly inspect and maintain perimeter barriers to address any damage or vulnerabilities.

6. Use Shatterproof Glass: Upgrading to shatterproof glass for windows and doors minimizes the risk of vandalism by making it more difficult for vandals to break into the building.

- Consider laminated or tempered glass for increased durability and resistance to impact.

- Install protective film coatings on existing glass surfaces as a cost-effective alternative to complete replacement.
- Evaluate the feasibility of reinforcing vulnerable entry points with security bars or grilles.

7. Partner with Local Law Enforcement: Establishing a collaborative relationship with local law enforcement agencies ensures prompt response and support in the event of vandalism or other security incidents.

- Arrange meetings with law enforcement officials to discuss security concerns and develop a coordinated response plan.
- Provide law enforcement with access to church premises for patrols or security checks during off-hours.
- Participate in community policing initiatives or neighborhood watch programs to strengthen ties with local authorities.

8. Conduct Regular Security Assessments: Regular security assessments help identify vulnerabilities and assess the effectiveness of existing security measures, allowing for proactive adjustments and improvements.

- Engage professional security consultants or conduct internal assessments using established guidelines or checklists.

- Involve staff, volunteers, and community members in the assessment process to gather diverse perspectives.
- Prioritize areas identified as high-risk or susceptible to vandalism for targeted security enhancements.

CHAPTER 26

Active Shooter Events: Preparation and Response

Active shooter events can happen anywhere and at any time. The latest community of faith impacted by this was Joel Osteen's church. Many perpetrators of these crimes view churches as soft targets, incapable of mounting a strong response to their onslaught. Within just two minutes, an active shooter on the loose with a semi-automatic weapon can wreak havoc in a room where several people are assembled. Given the fact that it takes somewhere between seven to nine minutes for law enforcement to arrive on the scene of these crimes, churches have a duty to prepare their members to respond in the event something like this should occur at their church.

There are several entities that have dedicated their services to helping organizations, including communities of faith, to mount a proactive response to active shooter events. For example, *ALICE, ALERT,* and *Run! Hide! Fight!* are all active shooter responses that will equip your members to not be passive responders to such a threat, but to do whatever is necessary to survive. There are several courses, certifications, and videos online that can be accessed to learn more about how to effectively respond to an active shooter event. We could go much deeper but here is a road map on where to begin:

Adopt an Active Shooter Response Plan: Churches should have a security plan that outlines procedures for protecting against and responding to acts of violence or terrorism. This plan should be developed in consultation with experts in the field of security and law enforcement. There are many response measures in place for active shooter events. The best response to active shooter events provides victims with a buffet of options that will increase their chances of survival. These include communicating clearly during a crisis, evacuating (this is the safest and best option if it is possible), fighting back as a last resort, and hiding if evacuating is not an option.

Training Staff and Volunteers: Churches should train their staff and volunteers on how to identify and respond to potentially violent threats. They should also incorporate relevant security protocols within these trainings, such as evacuation procedures, communication plans, and first aid practices. In our case, the services of a corporal from Prince Georges County Sheriff's Department who is a certified active shooter instructor were retained to lead our churches and schools in training, drills, and exercises that will help them build and retain muscle memory should an active shooter event take place within our facilities. We also invested in an age-appropriate curriculum for children to learn about the key response strategies, while not being traumatized by the actual events of a such heinous acts.

Evacuation: Leading churches in evacuation drills and exercises that will help them to create distance between themselves and the threat (once it is safe to do so) is a very important security measure that should be taken. Members should be aware of all exit points in their buildings and should be able to access them during an emergency. They should also be educated on the rally points or safe zone that they will all go to after an event, to be accounted for and to wait for law enforcement.

Armed Security at Church: Many insurance companies now offer limited liability coverage for churches in the case of a wrongful death incident. It is for this reason that we strongly encourage church leadership to only employ the services of law enforcement to provide armed security services. They are already licensed to use deadly force and will have certain levels of immunity and liability coverage for protecting the congregation. If a third-party security company is hired, it is highly recommended that they provide the church with proof of insurance that names the church as additionally insured and has appropriate coverage limits in keeping with your church policy.

I've seen scenarios in which some churches have engaged the services of congregants who are only licensed gun owners to perform this role, and this is strongly discouraged. Given the liability implications that can emerge, it can be catastrophic in the case of a wrongful death lawsuit.

In one of our churches, the leadership established a budget that pays a police officer to provide armed security at both of their worship services, which adds up to a total of five hours on a weekly basis. They pay these officers at a reasonable hourly rate to provide armed protection.

While it may not be practical for all churches to do this, I would urge those in leadership to discuss this with their insurance carrier to determine the level of coverage they have for armed security at church and make a decision on the best course of action to take.

Evaluate Access Points: Churches should evaluate their access points to identify potential weaknesses that could allow an attacker to enter the building. They should also consider installing security cameras, alarms, and other deterrents.

Communicating Clearly During an Attack: Considering recent security threats faced by organizations, there has been an increased focus on ensuring effective communication in emergency situations. One such measure that has gained popularity is the use of code words to alert building occupants of a threat. However, experts recommend clear and concise language instead of code words to communicate the threat effectively.

It is important to note that the use of code words can only help protect those who have been trained in their meaning, which may only be a select few volunteers and employees. This leaves a large portion of the building occupants uninformed and vulnerable in emergency situations. Therefore, clear, and concise language is the best practice measure now recommended.

Some may argue that the use of code words prevents panic. However, once there is a threat of an active shooter in the building, the panic element is already present. The primary goal at this point is to ensure that everyone in the building is aware of the location of the threat, empowering them to make decisions that will increase their chances of survival.

It is vital for organizations to prioritize effective communication in times of emergency. Clear and concise language is the most effective way to communicate the threat and ensure the safety of all building occupants.

Develop Response Protocols: Finally, churches should develop response protocols that can be implemented in case of a crisis. This can include establishing a chain of command, setting up a communication plan, and ensuring that congregants know what to do in case of an emergency.

By taking these steps, churches can prevent and reduce the impact of acts of violence or terrorism. While there is no way to eliminate the risk of such events, these measures can help to keep congregants safe and secure.

Guns and Weapons at Church

The issue of whether to allow firearms on church premises has become a subject of great debate among church officers. While the United States Constitution grants its citizens the right to bear arms, private properties such as churches have leeway in determining their own policies regarding weapons. It is the responsibility of church leaders to acquire knowledge on relevant laws concerning weapons and ensure that their decisions do not violate the Second Amendment rights of their congregation.

Laws surrounding firearms vary depending on the state. In some states, it is permissible to openly carry guns, while others dictate that firearms must be kept within the confines of the gun owner's home. Church officers must bear this in mind when formulating their policies on firearms on church-owned property.

Should a church opt to implement a no-firearms policy on its property, it must first adopt this resolution through an official decision by its governing board. Following this, it is essential for the church to effectively disseminate this policy to those attending services and any other individuals accessing the church facilities. Simply posting signs that ban firearms can inadvertently draw the attention of malicious individuals, especially if there is an absence of armed security personnel. Thus, the church should utilize alternative methods such as making routine announcements, posting in bulletins, and employing digital channels to communicate this crucial safety policy.

CHAPTER 27

Cyber Risk Awareness and Prevention

Shady Brook Church found itself in the throes of completing a construction project when a devastating phone call reached the project manager. The caller, John, the primary contractor, delivered grim news: payment hadn't been received as expected. The blow was profound because just a week and a half prior, the church accountant had confirmed via email that the payment had been wired to the contractor.

As they delved into the matter, it became evident that they had fallen victim to wire fraud. The accountant had received an email purportedly from a representative of the construction company, complete with the company's logo in the signature. The email, seemingly legitimate at the time, outlined changes in payment procedures, stating that instead of the usual printed check, a wire transfer was required for this instance. Without consulting the project manager, the accountant processed the wire transfer, leading to the church being scammed out of over one hundred thousand dollars.

As technology progressively becomes interwoven into every aspect of our lives, the threat of cyber-attacks looms larger than ever before. Unfortunately, stories like the one above demonstrate that churches are not immune to cybercrime. In fact, churches have become more attractive targets to cybercriminals due to their welcoming nature and to the access hackers can gain to financial and personal information databases.

Cyber-attacks come in many forms, such as ransomware, phishing, and wire fraud. These attacks can be financially devastating, but can also be emotionally distressing, especially when personal information such as addresses, phone numbers, and even Social Security numbers are compromised.

Given these alarming realities, it has become essential for churches to establish a comprehensive cyber risk prevention program. This program should be designed to identify potential risks, assess the vulnerabilities within the system, and provide strategies to mitigate these risks. Such programs will allow churches to better protect sensitive information, preserve their reputation, and safeguard their resources.

A church in Texas fell victim to a cyber-attack that resulted in the theft of personal and financial information of its members. The hackers exploited a vulnerability in the church's online payment system and stole credit card information, Social Security numbers, and personal addresses. The church was not only held liable for any unauthorized purchases made by the cybercriminals but also suffered immense reputational damage, which was challenging to overcome.

Another church was a victim of a ransomware attack that demanded thousands of dollars to be paid to the hackers to regain control of their data. The church's database was encrypted, disabling all access to important files and documents. The church was forced to pay the ransom, which was a considerable financial burden. Furthermore, the attack left the congregation feeling uneasy and worried about the security of their personal information.

These stories illustrate the severe consequences that can result from cyber-attacks. By establishing a comprehensive cyber risk prevention program, churches can ensure they are better equipped to identify potential threats, mitigate risks, and respond effectively in the event of an attack. Through the adoption of essential security measures, such as education and awareness training, simulated phishing campaigns, and adopting risk management standards for cyber security, churches can become more resilient against cyber-attacks. It is essential for churches to develop and implement such programs to safeguard their members and resources, and to preserve their mission and values.

Adopting a Risk Management Standard for Cyber Risk Response

Cyber-attacks pose a serious threat to churches and religious organizations of all sizes. With the increasing frequency and sophistication of cyber threats, it's imperative for churches to develop a comprehensive cyber risk prevention strategy that includes risk management standards. Risk management standards are a set of guidelines and procedures that organizations can follow to mitigate risks and prevent cyberattacks.

ISO/IEC 27001

One widely used standard is the ISO/IEC 27001. This standard outlines a risk management framework that covers the entire information security management system. It includes requirements for risk assessment, risk treatment, and risk monitoring. Additionally, it provides guidelines on the implementation and maintenance of an information security management system (ISMS). By following this standard, churches can ensure the confidentiality, integrity, and availability of their critical information assets.

National Institute of Standards and Technology Cybersecurity Framework (NIST)

Another important standard is the National Institute of Standards and Technology (NIST) Cybersecurity Framework. This framework provides a set of guidelines and best practices for organizations to manage and reduce cybersecurity risks. It's designed to help organizations identify, assess, manage, and respond to cybersecurity risks in a cost-effective and flexible manner. The NIST framework includes five core functions: Identify, Protect, Detect, Respond, and Recover. By following the framework, churches can strengthen their cybersecurity posture and reduce the likelihood and impact of cyberattacks.

Cyber risk prevention strategies should include risk management standards to ensure that organizations are adequately prepared to prevent, detect, and respond to cyber threats. These standards provide a framework for organizations to mitigate risks and protect their critical assets and data. By adopting these standards, organizations can enhance their overall cybersecurity posture and reduce the likelihood of experiencing a costly and damaging cyberattack.

Education and Awareness

Cyber criminals have become more sophisticated, threatening the fundamental value of confidentiality, integrity, and availability of business, financial, and personal information. As a result, it is essential to empower employees and volunteers with knowledge and training to identify, prevent, and respond to cyber threats.

The importance of cyber risk education and awareness programs cannot be overstated. Churches and other religious institutions have a lot to lose if they fail to take the necessary steps to protect their data from cyber threats. A single data breach could potentially bring an organization to its knees, jeopardizing its reputation, financial stability, and ability to carry out its mission.

One effective approach to educating employees and volunteers about cyber risks is with short animated videos. Such videos, like those provided by Ninjio, are highly engaging and informative, providing critical strategies for avoiding the traps of cyber attackers. The use of these simple yet effective tools fosters a culture of vigilance and awareness that helps reinforce critical knowledge that can go a long way in improving defense against cyber-attacks.

However, the significance of cyber risk education and awareness programs extends beyond the immediate benefits of preventing data breaches. These programs promote increased collaboration among teams, helping to develop a sense of shared responsibility for cybersecurity. Additionally, they improve the effectiveness of the organization's cybersecurity program by equipping employees with best practices that they can apply to their day-to-day activities.

Cyber risk education and awareness programs should be a crucial component of every church's cybersecurity response. By keeping employees and volunteers informed about emerging threats, prevention strategies, and best practices, churches can prevent data breaches and foster a culture of cybersecurity. Therefore, churches and other religious institutions should take proactive steps to invest in high-quality training programs that equip their teams with knowledge to safeguard against cyber threats.

Cyber Risk Insurance

Procuring cyber risk insurance is not merely an option for churches; it's a necessity in today's digital landscape. The ramifications of a cyber-attack can extend far beyond financial loss, potentially compromising sensitive data, eroding trust within the congregation, and disrupting vital services. In the face of such threats, having the right insurance coverage can provide a crucial safety net, offering financial protection and peace of mind to church leaders and members alike.

However, navigating the terrain of cyber risk insurance can pose significant challenges for churches. Unlike traditional insurance policies, which may be more straightforward to obtain, cyber risk insurance policies often come with stringent requirements and standards that must be met. Churches must demonstrate a robust cybersecurity posture, including measures such as firewalls, antivirus software, data encryption, employee training programs, and incident response plans. Meeting these standards can be particularly challenging for smaller congregations with limited resources and expertise in cybersecurity.

Furthermore, the landscape of cyber risk insurance for churches is characterized by a limited number of carriers specializing in this niche market. With fewer options available, competition is reduced, and premiums may be higher as a result. Churches may find themselves grappling with the dilemma of balancing their budget constraints with the need for adequate insurance coverage. Additionally, some carriers may be hesitant to underwrite policies for churches due to perceived higher risk factors, such as the potential for data breaches or ransomware attacks.

Despite these challenges, churches must persevere in their quest to procure cyber risk insurance. Partnering with knowledgeable insurance brokers who understand the unique needs and vulnerabilities of religious organizations can be instrumental in navigating this complex process. By investing in cybersecurity measures and seeking out reputable insurance providers, churches can safeguard their sacred spaces and protect the invaluable trust of their congregations in an increasingly digital world.

How Vulnerable Are We?

Considering the long-term impact that cyber-attacks can have on churches, the question "How vulnerable are we?" becomes a very important one in mounting an effective response to sinister intent of these bad actors. Assessing your church's vulnerability to cyber-attacks can take the form of:

1. Hiring an expert to look at your IT infrastructure or your website to identify system vulnerabilities.
2. Conducting simulated phishing exercises for employees and volunteers to identify individuals who are at risk for cyber-attacks.

Testing and diagnosing your church's systems for vulnerabilities is the first step in transforming your organization into a hard target. You need to identify any weaknesses in your system that could allow hackers to gain access to your information. Once identified, immediate steps should be taken to address these vulnerabilities.

Implementing strict security protocols, generating regular back-ups of sensitive information, and incorporating multi-factor authentication measures can significantly enhance the security of your church's systems.

Churches are becoming increasingly susceptible to cyber threats as technology continues to grow, and that's why it's necessary to test and diagnose their systems' vulnerabilities. Regular testing and diagnosis of your organization's information systems cannot be overemphasized because it helps detect any potential areas of weakness that may be exploited by hackers. By doing so, you can take the necessary steps to transform your church organization into a hard target.

Creating a comprehensive checklist to evaluate the vulnerabilities that a church may have to cyber-attacks involves assessing various aspects of its digital infrastructure, processes, and personnel. A structured checklist has been provided for you in the appendix of this book. Feel free to use it as a great starting point for evaluating your cyber risk vulnerability. By systematically evaluating these areas of vulnerability, churches can identify potential weaknesses in their cybersecurity posture and take proactive measures to strengthen their defenses against cyber-attacks. Regular assessments and reviews should be conducted to adapt to evolving threats and ensure ongoing protection of sensitive information and digital assets.

CHAPTER 28

Protecting the Funds: Fraud Prevention at Church

Fraud prevention is an important topic that deserves careful consideration within any organization, including religious institutions such as churches. Fraud is generally understood as an illegal act or deception carried out by an individual or group to gain financial or personal advantage.

Fraud can occur in a variety of ways, from misappropriation of funds to falsification of financial statements. Therefore, it is essential for churches to implement proper fraud prevention measures to protect their resources and the trust of their members.

One of the pitfalls that religious organizations face is the handling of restricted funds. One church found itself in the middle of a scandal when it was discovered that funds designated for a specific purpose had been misappropriated by the church leadership. The congregation had generously donated a substantial sum to create a scholarship fund to support underprivileged youth in the community with their educational expenses. However, investigations revealed that the church leadership had been diverting a portion of these funds to cover operational expenses and personal expenditures unrelated to the intended purpose.

As the news broke, outrage spread among the congregation and the broader community, tarnishing the church's reputation and eroding trust in its leadership. Concerned members demanded transparency and accountability, prompting a thorough investigation into the mismanagement of funds. External auditors were brought in to conduct a forensic audit, uncovering the extent of the financial misappropriation and identifying individuals responsible for the misuse of restricted funds.

In response to the findings, the church leadership issued a public apology and pledged to rectify the situation. Restitution was made to the scholarship fund, with additional measures implemented to ensure proper financial oversight and accountability moving forward. Those found culpable were held accountable through disciplinary actions, including resignations and legal consequences.

To rebuild trust and demonstrate a commitment to integrity, this church embarked on a series of transparency initiatives, including regular financial reporting to the congregation, enhanced internal controls, and the establishment of an independent oversight committee to monitor fund allocation and expenditure. Through these measures, the church took proactive steps to address the wrongdoing, restore confidence among its members, and reaffirm its commitment to stewardship and ethical conduct.

Addressing the Fraud Triangle

One of the key concepts in fraud prevention is the "fraud triangle." According to the Association of Certified Fraud Examiners (ACFE), the three critical factors that contribute to fraudulent activities are opportunity, rationalization, and pressure. The fraud triangle is a model that explains these three essential elements necessary for fraud to occur. Simply put, fraud can only occur if there is an opportunity for it, the person committing the fraud can justify it in their mind, and they feel pressure to do it.

Opportunity is the first facet of the fraud triangle, as it is the starting point for most fraud. The opportunity for fraud arises due to a lack of proper internal controls in the organization. Churches frequently lack proper internal controls or may not have enough checks and balances in place, making them vulnerable to fraud.

Rationalization is the second factor in the fraud triangle, in which the fraudster justifies their behavior and convinces themselves that their actions are morally or ethically acceptable. In the case of church fraud, the internal fraudster may rationalize their actions by claiming to have financial troubles or believing they deserve more compensation.

The final factor in the fraud triangle is pressure.

Pressure is the driving force that pushes an individual towards committing fraud. This could be due to personal financial struggles, addiction, or mounting debt. Wherever the loopholes exist within any one of these three elements, it is an area of vulnerability and proactive steps should be taken to prevent such an occurrence. For example, in some churches, everyone who serves in the treasury is required to submit to background checks and credit report screening.

It is essential to address the fraud triangle to prevent fraud from occurring within a church setting. This involves implementing appropriate internal controls such as background checks for employees and volunteers, requiring financial training for key personnel, and regular audits of the church's finances. Additionally, churches must prioritize an ethical culture that discourages fraudulent behavior, regularly communicates the importance of honesty and transparency, and encourages reporting of suspicious behavior.

Preventative Measures

To mitigate these risks, churches can implement internal controls that limit opportunities for fraud and reduce the likelihood of it occurring. Internal controls include policies and procedures established by the church to protect its assets, ensure accuracy in financial reporting, and promote compliance with laws and regulations.

One way to establish internal controls is through the selection of treasurers or CFOs for positions of trust. The selection process should be based on objective criteria, such as their qualifications, experience, and references. It is also important to conduct background checks and verify the credentials of potential candidates.

Handling Cash at Church

Safeguarding cash at churches is crucial to maintain transparency, accountability, and to prevent any potential mismanagement or theft of the offerings collected during the service. Here are several measures that churches can implement to handle cash effectively:

1. Select Trustworthy Deacons and Ushers: Ensure that individuals responsible for handling cash, such as deacons and ushers, are trustworthy and have undergone background checks. Select individuals who have a track record of honesty and integrity within the church community.

2. Require Two or More People to Count Funds: Implement a policy where at least two individuals, preferably more, count the funds collected during services. This dual-control method helps to minimize the risk of errors or misconduct, as well as provide accountability.

3. Secure Collection Boxes or Bags: Use secure collection boxes or bags that can be sealed and locked to prevent tampering or unauthorized access to the offerings. These boxes should only be opened by designated personnel during the counting process.

4. **Maintain Proper Documentation:** Keep detailed records of all offerings collected, including the date, amount, and purpose of the donation. This documentation not only ensures transparency but also aids in tracking and reconciliation.

5. **Implement Petty Cash Monitoring:** If petty cash is used for church expenses, establish strict guidelines for its usage and regularly monitor its disbursement and replenishment. Assign a designated individual to oversee petty cash transactions and require receipts for all expenditures.

6. **Vigilance During Bank Deposits:** Remain vigilant when making bank deposits by using secure transportation methods and varying deposit times to avoid predictability. Ensure that deposits are promptly recorded and reconciled with the corresponding offerings collected.

7. **Encourage Online Donations:** Encourage congregation members to utilize online donation platforms or electronic fund transfers to contribute their offerings. This helps to minimize the amount of cash handled at the church and provides a secure and convenient alternative for donors.

Furthermore, churches should ensure that there is proper segregation of duties, which means that no one person has control over all aspects of financial operations. This can include having different individuals responsible for receiving and depositing funds, paying bills, reconciling bank statements, and preparing financial reports.

Another key aspect of fraud prevention is maintaining a culture of integrity and ethical behavior. This can be achieved through establishing a code of conduct that clearly outlines the expectations for employees and volunteers and providing training and education on ethical decision-making.

CHAPTER 29

Should We Rent or Should We Buy?

When considering whether to buy or rent a building for church activities, it is important to weigh the pros and cons of both options. While purchasing a property may seem like a wise long-term investment, it is important to acknowledge that affording a church is more than being able to pay the mortgage.

One key factor to consider is the importance of preventative maintenance issues. As a church, it is crucial to maintain a safe and welcoming environment for congregants. Building upkeep and repairs can be costly and time-consuming, and neglecting them can lead to safety hazards and costly repairs in the future.

When renting a building, the responsibility of maintenance largely falls on the property owner. This removes the burden of upkeep from the church and allows for more time and resources to be dedicated to ministry activities. Additionally, renting may offer more flexibility in terms of location and size, allowing for the ability to easily transition to a larger or more convenient space as needs change.

However, renting also comes with its own set of challenges. Landlords may have specific requirements or restrictions that limit the church's ability to make necessary changes, such as updating the space to better accommodate ministry programs. Additionally, the cost of rent may increase over time and become a significant financial burden.

Purchasing a property offers the benefit of ownership and the potential for long-term financial gain. It also allows for complete control over the space and the ability to make necessary changes without relying on a landlord's approval. However, the initial cost of purchasing a property and the ongoing expenses of maintenance and repairs can be a significant strain on the church's finances.

Both options have their advantages and disadvantages, and it is important to carefully consider the specific needs and goals of the church before deciding. Ultimately, the decision to buy or rent a building for church activities should be made after a thorough assessment of the financial and practical considerations involved to ensure effective risk management for the church.

Lessor's Risk: Leveraging Church Facilities while Balancing Revenue and Risks

Lately, as financial sustainability is a pressing concern for many religious institutions, the notion of leasing church facilities to external entities is a viable strategy to help churches in this regard. This section explores the benefits and challenges inherent in this approach, while shedding light on how lessors risk insurance can safeguard churches and their ministries from potential threats.

Benefits of Leasing Out Church Facilities

Financial Stability: Leasing out church facilities presents a significant opportunity for generating supplemental revenue streams. These funds can be allocated towards various operational expenses, community outreach programs, or facility maintenance projects, ultimately bolstering the financial health of the congregation.

Community Engagement: By opening their doors to external organizations, churches can foster greater community engagement and collaboration. Whether hosting local businesses, non-profit organizations, or cultural events, these partnerships cultivate a sense of inclusivity and shared purpose within the neighborhood.

Resource Optimization: Utilizing church facilities during non-traditional hours or days can maximize their utility and value. By leasing out spaces that would otherwise remain idle, churches can optimize their resources and ensure that their assets are utilized to their fullest potential.

Challenges of Leasing Church Facilities

Risk Exposure: Entrusting church premises to external parties inevitably introduces a degree of risk. From property damage to liability claims arising from accidents or disputes, churches must navigate potential hazards associated with leasing their facilities.

Maintaining Sacred Spaces: Balancing the commercial use of church facilities with the preservation of their sacred purpose can pose a challenge. Striking a harmonious balance between generating revenue and upholding the spiritual integrity of the space requires careful consideration and planning.

Legal and Regulatory Compliance: Churches must adhere to relevant legal and regulatory frameworks when leasing their facilities. Navigating zoning laws, building codes, and contractual obligations demands meticulous attention to detail to avoid potential legal pitfalls.

Lessor's Risk Insurance: Protecting Church Ministries

Lessor's risk insurance serves as a critical safeguard against the myriad risks associated with leasing church facilities. This specialized form of coverage provides financial protection in the event of property damage, bodily injury claims, or legal liabilities arising from third-party use of the premises. Here are some key features of lessor's risk insurance.

Property Protection: Coverage extends to the physical structure of the church and its contents, shielding against perils such as fire, vandalism, or theft. In the event of property damage, the insurance policy facilitates prompt repairs or replacements, minimizing disruptions to church operations.

Liability Coverage: Lessor's risk insurance provides liability protection against claims brought forth by third parties, including tenants, visitors, or event attendees. Whether it's a slip-and-fall accident or property damage caused by a lessee, the policy safeguards the church from costly legal proceedings and settlements.

Customizable Options: Churches can tailor their lessor's risk insurance policies to suit their specific needs and risk profiles. By consulting with experienced insurance providers, congregations can assess their exposure levels and procure coverage that aligns with their leasing activities and financial capabilities.

Leasing church facilities to external entities offers a strategic avenue for revenue generation and community engagement. However, churches must remain vigilant in mitigating associated risks through comprehensive risk management strategies, including the procurement of lessor's risk insurance.

Section IV: Protecting the Reputation of Your Ministry

CHAPTER 30

Managing the Reputation of Your Ministry

While physical and financial assets are important to the day-to-day missional operations of your church, there remains a very important pillar in the longevity and success of your ministry—an impeccable reputation. In the corporate world, this is also referred to as "brand equity."

For religious organizations, the importance of reputation within the ministry cannot be overstated. A church's reputation serves as a foundational pillar upon which its influence, credibility, and ability to fulfill its mission are built. Reputation, in the context of a church, extends far beyond mere public perception; it encapsulates the collective trust, respect, and goodwill that the congregation, the broader community, and society at large attribute to the religious institution. This intangible asset is cultivated through years of consistent ethical conduct, compassionate outreach, and steadfast adherence to the principles and values espoused by the faith.

The reputation of a church is a multifaceted concept, encompassing both the spiritual and practical dimensions of its existence. Spiritually, it reflects the church's commitment to upholding moral and ethical standards, fostering a sense of community, and providing spiritual guidance to its members.

Practically, it involves how the church engages with its surrounding community, responds to societal issues, and manages its internal affairs. A positive reputation enhances the church's ability to attract and retain members, collaborate with other community organizations, and serve as a beacon of hope and support for individuals seeking spiritual fulfillment.

Moreover, a church's reputation carries implications for its outreach efforts, influencing its capacity to carry out charitable initiatives, promote social justice, and contribute positively to the well-being of the community it serves. In an era marked by information abundance and interconnectedness, a church's reputation is not confined to the physical walls of its sanctuary; it resonates across digital platforms, social media, and various communication channels, shaping public perception in real time.

The Role of Church Officers in Safeguarding the Reputation of the Church

Serving as a church officer with board responsibilities is a weighty role that carries significant implications for the preservation and safeguarding of a religious organization's reputation. The individuals entrusted with such positions are often the stewards of the church's mission, values, and ethical standards. They play a pivotal role in setting the tone for the entire congregation, ensuring that the actions and decisions of the church align with its core principles. As custodians of the organization's governance, church leaders are instrumental in maintaining transparency, accountability, and integrity within the church community.

One of the primary functions of church officers with board responsibilities is to establish and enforce policies that promote ethical behavior and responsible stewardship of resources. By fostering a culture of accountability, these leaders contribute to the creation of an environment where trust and credibility flourish. This, in turn, serves to fortify the reputation of the religious organization not only among its members but also within the broader community. The actions and decisions of church officers are often scrutinized, and their commitment to upholding ethical standards becomes a visible manifestation of the church's dedication to its principles.

Moreover, church officers with board responsibilities are instrumental in navigating complex challenges and controversies that may arise. Their leadership in times of crisis can be decisive in mitigating reputational risks and steering the organization through tumultuous waters. By adhering to transparent communication, swift and ethical decision-making, and a commitment to resolving conflicts with fairness and compassion, these officers contribute significantly to the resilience and longevity of the church's positive reputation. In essence, their role extends beyond the administrative realm; it is a sacred trust that, when fulfilled with integrity, enhances the credibility and enduring influence of the religious organization they serve.

There are several factors that can have a profound impact on the reputation of churches. In this next section, we will focus on some of the more common reputational risks:

1. Mismanagement of crises
2. Financial mismanagement
3. Legal issues
4. Moral and ethical scandals
5. Negative online presence (social edia etc.)
6. Leadership controversy
7. Doctrinal or theological disputes

CHAPTER 31

Managing Crisis with Effective Communication

The mismanagement of crises can cast a shadow that reverberates far beyond the physical walls of a church. Natural disasters, accidents, and unforeseen emergencies pose unique challenges that demand a coordinated and compassionate response from religious institutions.

This chapter delves into the critical dimensions of crisis mismanagement within faith communities, shedding light on the consequences of an inability to effectively manage and communicate during tumultuous times. From the chaos of natural calamities to the unforeseen accidents that shake the foundations of faith, the repercussions of inadequate preparation become starkly evident.

Crisis Communication Strategies

A poorly handled crisis can quickly tarnish the image of a church and negatively impact the community it serves. With the rise of social media and the twenty-four-hour news cycle, misinformation around a crisis can spread like wildfire. That's why it's essential for churches to have a crisis communication strategy in place.

A crisis communication strategy is a crucial component of any risk management program. It provides a framework for a church to effectively communicate during a crisis and mitigate damage to its reputation. This strategy should include a thorough understanding of the different types of crises that a church may face, as well as clear and concise communication plans for each scenario.

A comprehensive crisis communication strategy should also designate individuals to take on specific roles in times of crisis, as well as establish communication protocols for the dissemination of information to key stakeholders. In addition, the strategy should include plans for monitoring and responding to social media activity and media inquiries.

Without a well-executed crisis communication strategy, a church may struggle to respond to a crisis in a timely and effective manner, leading to further damage to its reputation and credibility. In today's world, the importance of an efficient and effective crisis communication strategy cannot be overstated.

In the following sections, we will delve deeper into the best practices for developing a crisis communication strategy for your church, including essential elements, key roles, and effective communication techniques that will help protect your church's reputation and restore trust in the wake of a crisis.

Developing a Crisis Communication Plan

When developing a crisis communication plan for a church, it is important to ensure an effective and timely response to any potential crisis. Here is a step-by-step breakdown on how to accomplish this.

Step 1: Organize a Crisis Communication Team. Identify individuals within the church who will form a crisis communication team. This team should be made up of individuals who have various skills and responsibilities, including leadership, communication, administration, and technology. The team should meet regularly to discuss potential scenarios and what steps to take in each case.

Step 2: Identify Potential Crises. Determine the possible crises that a church may face, such as data breaches, fraud, scandals involving pastors, medical emergencies, criminal activity, or damage to church property. Each scenario should be evaluated, and a response plan developed for each event.

Step 3: Develop a Crisis Response Plan. Create a step-by-step plan to respond to each potential crisis, such as evacuation procedures, emergency messaging, and any necessary liaisons with emergency services. Determine who will be responsible for executing each plan.

Step 4: Establish a Communication Strategy. Create a communication strategy that includes a plan to inform members of the church, the community, and the media about the crisis. Identify the most appropriate communication channels, such as email, text messages or social media, and create message templates beforehand.

Step 5: Train the Crisis Communication Team. It is important to make sure that the crisis communication team members are properly trained on their roles and responsibilities in a crisis. They should be able to implement the crisis response plan and communicate with calm assurance in a high-pressure situation quickly and effectively.

Step 6: Review and Update the Plan Regularly. A crisis communication plan should be reviewed regularly, and updates made as necessary, to accommodate changes in circumstances, church infrastructure, and communication methods.

A crisis communication plan is a vital tool for a church to ensure the safety and well-being of its members and provide effective communication in the face of a crisis. By following these steps, a church will have a well-organized and proactive approach to dealing with various emergencies.

Handling Media Relations During Challenging Times

Handling media relations during challenging times for churches can be a daunting task. However, it is crucial to ensure that your organization maintains transparency, demonstrates accountability, and manages expectations. The right approach will not only help you to manage news coverage but also help to preserve your organization's reputation.

To help handle media relations during challenging times, the following step-by-step breakdown can be valuable.

Establish a Media Protocol: If the crisis communication plan is in place as discussed in the previous section, churches should have a media protocol that outlines how they interact with the media, who the designated spokesperson is, and how to handle inquiries from the media. This document should be updated regularly and provide instructions for managing sensitive information and communicating with different stakeholders during a crisis.

Activate a Crisis Communication Team: This is not a drill. Whereas the communication plan requires scenario-based activity, this is the time for all that practice to be put into action. In many cases, stand-alone churches have a dedicated team that will be responsible for handling media relations, whereas, in other instances, there is a centralized office where someone from that location is the primary contact. The important thing is for each member of the team to be trained on what steps are to be taken when dealing with the media and have a keen understanding of church values, the community, and stakeholders' expectations.

Develop Key Messages: During a crisis, clarity in messaging is of utmost importance. The communication team should be equipped with key messages to use when communicating with the media and other stakeholders. They should be factual, concise, consistent, and focused on addressing the crisis.

Leverage the Power of Social Media: Social media platforms can be excellent tools to manage church media relations during a crisis. You can use platforms like X (Twitter), Facebook, Instagram, and LinkedIn to provide frequent updates, answer frequently asked questions, and engage with the public.

Arrange Press Conferences: Press conferences are an excellent way to get important information out to a vast audience, including the media. They allow for questions and give a deeper insight into the crisis, allowing the media to present accurate and balanced coverage.

Follow up with the Media: It's important to follow up with the media immediately after a press conference or any interaction to ensure that they have accurate information. This approach will help to minimize any misconceptions or misinformation that may create more negative media coverage.

Develop a Strategy for Employee Protection: If the crisis in question is related to an employee, there are different privacy and employee laws that may apply. When handling sensitive information concerning an employee, it's imperative to follow a protocol that protects the employee's privacy and welfare while also managing the church's reputation.

Churches must have a detailed plan in place for handling media during difficult times. This plan should include a designated team, a media protocol manual, social media strategy, and proactive communication with employees, stakeholders, and the media. A well-executed media relations strategy can prevent negative coverage, protect the church's image, and foster a sense of trust with stakeholders.

CHAPTER 32

Responding to Financial Scandals

The management of financial resources is not just a matter of fiscal responsibility; it is an ethical imperative that shapes the perception of the entire faith-based community. This section delves into the profound impact of financial mismanagement on the reputation of faith-based organizations, illuminating the consequences that arise from the improper handling of church finances, the lack of transparency in financial reporting, and the failure to meet financial obligations, like paying bills or debts.

When we consider that all faith-based communities are donor-funded, it behooves church leaders to take very seriously their role in ensuring that their churches are being fiscally responsible. Those who choose to donate to your ministry do so because they believe in your mission enough to invest in it. These sacred resources are to be managed in a manner worthy of that trust.

As a church, your reputation is everything. It's your credibility, trustworthiness, and reliability in the eyes of your members, community, and donors. However, it only takes a financial mismanagement scandal to put it all at risk. If not managed effectively, a scandal can damage your church's reputation and create a ripple effect that can last for years. As such, it's worth exploring how to effectively manage a church's reputation during a financial mismanagement scandal.

Embracing Honesty and Transparency

It's important to be transparent and honest. Donors want to know what's happened and how it's been addressed. Don't try to cover up or hide the issue. Instead, take ownership of the situation and provide information as soon as possible. Be open and honest about what's being done to resolve the crisis and prevent it from happening again in the future.

Establish a Crisis Communication Plan

Identify key stakeholders, designated spokespersons, internal communication channels, and protocols for communicating with the media and social media. Ensure that everyone involved in handling the situation is aware of the plan and is prepared to execute it at a moment's notice.

Demonstrate a commitment to accountability and responsible stewardship. This involves setting up systems and controls to prevent future mismanagement. Additionally, it means dedicating resources to accountability and transparency measures like independent audits, regular financial reporting, and donor communication tools.

Strive to demonstrate an organizational culture of ethics and integrity. This involves setting a tone at the top where ethical behavior is the norm, not the exception. Church leaders should model ethical behavior and encourage it throughout the community. They should also create an environment where employees feel comfortable reporting any ethical violations they witness.

Managing a church's reputation during a financial mismanagement scandal requires a proactive and comprehensive approach. By being transparent, establishing a crisis communications plan, demonstrating a commitment to accountability and responsible stewardship, and promoting an organizational culture of ethics and integrity, you can rebuild trust and safeguard your church's reputation.

CHAPTER 33

Managing Social Media and Online Presence

As the world becomes increasingly digitized, ministries and churches must adapt to new forms of outreach and connection. Social media presents one such opportunity. While there are certainly pitfalls to using social media, such as the potential for division or distraction from the mission, it is nonetheless a powerful tool for sharing the gospel, connecting people with each other, and growing a church community.

To effectively manage a church's social media presence, there must be a clear content creation strategy, responsible access and safeguarding of accounts, and a protocol for ensuring that all posted content aligns with the organization's strategic and missional objectives.

By utilizing social media in a responsible way, churches can more effectively engage with members and non-members alike, sharing the love of Christ and building meaningful relationships. In this chapter, we will explore the key principles and best practices for managing a church's social media presence.

Managing the Church's Online Reputation

Managing the church's online reputation is becoming increasingly important in today's digital age. Thanks to social media and other online communication tools, churches can reach out to their congregants and grow their network. However, with this opportunity comes the risk of negative feedback, bad reviews, and criticism. Therefore, it's crucial for churches to effectively manage their online reputation to safeguard their image and foster a positive online community.

One of the ways to manage the church's online reputation is by having a strong social media presence. Social media platforms such as Facebook, X (Twitter), Instagram, and LinkedIn provide churches with the opportunity to connect with people from all over the world. When used wisely, these platforms can help churches to create strong networks of online followers, which can help with everything from fundraising to promoting events and spreading the gospel.

Churches also need to monitor their social media accounts and respond promptly to messages, comments, and inquiries from followers. Regular communication with followers can help build trust and strengthen relationships with them. Consistent updates about church activities, sermons, and outreach efforts will help keep followers engaged and invested in the church's mission.

Another essential aspect of managing the church's online reputation is to proactively protect against reputational damage. This means creating risk management plans and protocols that will mitigate the risk of negative exposure online. Regularly monitoring online reviews and feedback will help ensure that any negative comments or posts are addressed promptly. In addition, establishing protocols for responding to negative comments can help prevent further escalation and protect the church's reputation.

A strong social media presence, regular communication with followers, and effective risk management practices can help safeguard the church's image and promote a positive online community. By investing time and resources into managing their online reputation, churches can create a welcoming and inclusive community that fosters personal growth, engagement, and spiritual connection.

Navigating Potential Risks Associated with Social Media for Churches

As mentioned before, while social media has now become a way of life and is a great way to perform online evangelism, it is without doubt that this technology also comes with potential risks that can harm the reputation of your church. Here are some potential risks associated with social media for churches and how to navigate them:

1. Privacy and data security
2. Cyberbullying and online harassment
3. Misuse of social media
4. Sexting, online predators, and child safety issues

Privacy and Data Security

In recent times, data breaches and identity theft have become increasingly common. Unfortunately, churches are not immune to these potential risks, especially when utilizing social media platforms. Therefore, it is essential for churches to take the necessary steps to protect their members' and leaders' personal information.

One critical aspect of data security is the use of secure passwords. It is crucial to use a unique password for each account and avoid using simple or common passwords. Additionally, regularly changing passwords and not sharing them with others can further strengthen the security of sensitive data.

Finally, churches can also employ technical measures to safeguard their data. Utilizing secure email services, encrypting data transfers, and implementing firewalls can all contribute to a more secure digital environment.

Cyberbullying and Online Harassment

Navigating potential risks associated with social media for churches requires understanding and addressing the risks of cyberbullying and online harassment. Cyberbullying refers to bullying behavior that takes place online or through electronic devices. Online harassment refers to any threatening or intimidating behavior that someone experiences online, which may include cyberbullying.

Cyberbullying and online harassment can result in emotional distress and mental health issues, and they can severely impact an individual's well-being. Unfortunately, these behaviors are increasingly prevalent online, and communities of faith also experience this. This makes it crucial for churches to establish clear social media guidelines and codes of conduct for both church leaders and members.

By establishing clear guidelines for social media use, churches can help prevent cyberbullying and online harassment. These guidelines should emphasize the importance of respectful communication and behavior, especially when interacting with others online. Leaders should impress upon their members to be responsible digital disciples, who are actively representing Christ in their online comments and interactions. By promoting a culture of respect and understanding online, churches can help create a safe and positive virtual environment. For example, certain comments and posts made on their social media platform can and should be deleted if they breach established codes of conduct, values, and norms for the church.

It is important to recognize that achieving absolute control over what others choose to post on social media platforms may prove challenging. However, an effective approach in mitigating risk is exercising control over what content remains posted on your page. This requires constant monitoring of social media activities, with a keen eye for identifying cyberbullying. It is imperative that any instance of cyberbullying is promptly highlighted and removed to minimize the harm caused to the victim and mitigate any repetition of this activity.

In some cases, it may become necessary to take more drastic measures. This may involve blocking individuals from commenting, particularly in circumstances where they have repeatedly failed to adhere to the policies governing that platform. Such actions should not be taken lightly, but rather as a proactive measure to prevent further harm and protect the integrity of the platform.

Churches should also monitor their social media pages to ensure that they remain safe and respectful spaces. This includes promptly responding to abusive comments and removing any content that violates the guidelines. Additionally, it is essential to provide support to anyone who has been a victim of cyberbullying or online harassment. This can include counseling services or support groups, as well as resources for reporting the behavior to relevant authorities.

Cyberbullying and online harassment are significant risks associated with social media use for churches. By establishing clear social media guidelines and codes of conduct, and monitoring online behavior, churches can help create a safe and positive virtual environment. Additionally, providing support to those impacted by online harassment is crucial to reducing the negative effects of cyberbullying.

Misuse of Social Media

There is the risk of social media being used to spread false information or misinformation, which can harm the credibility of the church and result in negative publicity. Churches should appoint responsible and trustworthy administrators to manage their social media pages and verify the authenticity of the information they post prior to doing so.

Sexting, Online Predators, and Child Safety

Social media poses a particular risk to young members of the church, as they may be vulnerable to online predators and sexting. Churches must implement policies and procedures that protect their younger members, such as closing direct messaging features or limiting interactions with strangers. Churches should also encourage parents to monitor their children's social media use and educate them on the potential dangers.

While social media offers churches great opportunities to connect with their members and the wider audience, it also poses various potential risks that require proper attention. By implementing robust social media guidelines, monitoring and responding appropriately to comments, and safeguarding sensitive data, churches can enjoy the benefits of social media while minimizing potential risks and protecting their members' safety and well-being.

CHAPTER 34

Conflict Resolution Within the Congregation

Conflict is an inherent aspect of every faith community, irrespective of its size or mission. Churches, too, face their share of challenges, as diverse personalities and varying beliefs among members often lead to disagreements and disputes. Unresolved conflicts have the potential to inflict lasting harm on a church's unity and spiritual development. In this regard, it becomes imperative for churches to prioritize conflict resolution and integrate it into their core mission. By employing effective strategies for conflict resolution, churches can foster peace and harmony within their congregation, enabling members to concentrate on their shared journey in embracing Christ's teachings and embodying His love.

Jesus capitalized on every opportunity to promote the peaceful resolution of conflict while He was on Earth. In fact, the biggest expectation for Him and His ministry was that He would lead a revolution against the Roman Empire to lift His people out of the oppressive regime. One of His beatitudes says, "God blesses those who work for peace, for they will be called the children of God" (Matthew 5:9).

Despite the biblical importance of conflict resolution in churches, many congregations struggle with this task. Often, conflicts are either ignored or dealt with haphazardly, leaving both parties feeling unheard and unsatisfied. In some cases, church leaders may not have the necessary skills or training to manage such situations, leading to further complications. Therefore, a comprehensive approach to resolving conflicts is crucial for churches to ensure that they are handling disputes systematically and effectively.

The good news is that conflict resolution is a skill that can be learned and developed. There are various techniques and approaches that churches can use to resolve disputes, including mediation, negotiation, and arbitration. By incorporating these methods into their conflict resolution plan, churches can create a safe and effective space for members to express their concerns and work towards a mutually beneficial resolution.

In this section, we will explore conflict resolution strategies that churches can use to manage disputes among their members. We will discuss the importance of effective communication, active listening, and empathy in resolving conflicts. We will also examine the role of church leaders in mediating disputes and the importance of creating a conflict resolution plan. By the end of this chapter, readers will have a better understanding of how to promote peace and harmony in their churches by effectively managing conflicts.

Addressing Internal Disputes with a Focus on Resolution

Addressing internal disputes within a church community can be a challenging and sensitive matter, but it is vital for maintaining healthy and harmonious relationships among members. Following is a step-by-step guide to resolving disputes within your community and promoting effective communication, active listening, and empathy.

Step 1: Acknowledge the Dispute

The first step in addressing internal disputes is to acknowledge that the dispute exists. You must empathize with the members involved and recognize the challenges they are facing. Don't dismiss conflict as a minor issue, as it can escalate further and hurt the community. Begin by reaching out to the parties involved and committing to a resolution.

Step 2: Identify the Root of the Problem

It is essential to identify the root cause of the dispute before attempting to resolve it. Encourage open communication between the parties involved to gain a deeper understanding of what led to the conflict. This step will help everyone to hear different perspectives and experiences.

Step 3: Encourage Listening and Empathy

As a leader, it is your responsibility to encourage the parties involved to listen to each other's side of the story. Promote active listening by asking questions and taking turns speaking. Create a safe environment where everyone feels heard, respected, and valued. Empathy is also required to promote a mutual understanding among the parties.

Step 4: Explore and Evaluate Possible Solutions

Once the parties have been heard and understood, work with them to explore various solutions and actions that can help them move forward. Encourage them to come up with their solutions so they can take ownership of them. Evaluate possible outcomes of each option. Discuss what will work best for everyone involved.

Step 5: Create a Conflict Resolution Plan

Together with the parties, create a conflict resolution plan that outlines the agreed-upon solutions, responsibilities, and timelines. This plan should be clear and comprehensive, covering all aspects of the resolution. It would be best to involve the parties in the development of the plan and ensure everyone understands it.

Step 6: Follow up and Review Progress

Once the conflict resolution plan is in place, it's vital to follow up regularly with the parties involved to check on the progress of the plan. Make yourself available to discuss any challenges that may arise. The success of the conflict resolution plan depends on the support it receives from all parties.

Resolving disputes within a church community requires effective communication, active listening, and empathy. By following the six steps outlined, you can help build a healthy, growing, and united community where everyone values and supports each other. Remember, addressing disputes is vital to the health and well-being of a church community, and as a leader, you must be proactive in finding ways to address conflicts.

CHAPTER 35

Preserving the Repuation of Your Ministry After a Scandal

Scandals within church leadership can shake the foundations of faith and trust in the institution. Here are examples of the types of scandals that churches may experience.

Sexual abuse: This type of scandal involves a member of the church leadership or staff engaging in sexually abusive behavior towards congregants, often minors. The Catholic Church has been particularly plagued by this issue, with numerous cases of abuse and cover-up coming to light in recent years.

Financial impropriety: This kind of scandal involves mismanagement or misuse of church funds. Instances of embezzlement, fraud, and lavish spending by church leaders have been reported in the past.

Political controversy: In some cases, church leaders may become embroiled in controversy related to political or social issues. For example, some churches have been criticized for their stance on LGBTQ+, abortion, or immigration.

Doctrinal disputes: Infighting over religious doctrine can lead to division within a church community. These disputes often arise when members of the congregation disagree with the direction that church leadership is taking.

Cover-ups and scandals within the leadership: The cover-up is often worse than the crime itself. When church leadership attempts to hide or obfuscate issues within their ranks, it can lead to a crisis of faith and trust among congregants.

In all cases, the fallout from church scandals can be severe, resulting in loss of membership, financial hardship, and damage to the reputation of the institution. It is essential for churches to hold their leadership accountable and transparent to prevent scandal from taking root.

When a church or its leaders are embroiled in any scandal, it has the potential to leave members feeling disillusioned and betrayed. The fallout from such a crisis can be devastating, not only for the individuals involved but for the entire ministry. In times of conflict, it is crucial to preserve the reputation of the church and its leadership.

It is essential that church leaders take proactive steps to protect the integrity of their ministry and the trust of their followers. This chapter will delve into the importance of preserving the reputation of the ministry during times of conflict and provide practical strategies that church leaders can employ to navigate crises with transparency, accountability, and integrity. Preserving the reputation of a ministry during times of conflict is critical to ensuring its continued success and relevance. Here's a step-by-step guide on how to maintain a good reputation during these turbulent times.

Address the issue head-on: The first step in preserving the reputation of a ministry during times of conflict is to address the issue head-on. Do not try to avoid or cover up the issue, as this will only amplify the problem and create more room for skeptics.

Communicate clearly with stakeholders: The second step is to communicate transparently with the stakeholders. Tell them what happened and what steps the ministry is taking to address the issue and its impact. Ensure stakeholders are aware of the steps taken to prevent a recurrence.

Apologize sincerely: If the issue was caused by the ministry's mistakes, it's important to apologize sincerely. Don't be vague or ambiguous about the apology, but own up to the mistake and apologize without placing blame on others.

Show genuine remorse: It's not only important to apologize, but to show genuine remorse for what has occurred. Show by your actions that the ministry is genuinely sorry for the impact of the scandal. Ensure that the ministry is taking steps to prevent instances of such scandal repeating.

Implement proactive measures: Commit yourself to implementing proactive measures that will ensure the issue never arises again. This step demonstrates that the ministry is serious about preventing future scandals and is working towards it proactively.

Continue to deliver the ministry's mission: Ensure that the ministry continues its mission to serve its community. This step ensures that the public can recognize that the ministry is still standing and committed to its purpose in the face of the scandal.

Be open to feedback: The final step involves being open to feedback. Accept constructive criticism regarding the ministry's leadership and processes. Act on that feedback to evaluate the ministry's leadership's effectiveness and organizational structure to prevent similar oversights in the future.

Preserving the ministry's reputation during times of conflict is critical to ensuring continued ministry success and relevance. By following these seven steps and taking measurable action, the ministry can emerge from the scandal with a renewed commitment and strengthened resolve.

CHAPTER 36

Legal Issues Affecting the Reputation of Your Church

We occasionally hear about religious organizations that find themselves entangled in illegal activities that have severely damaged their reputations and eroded public trust. From financial improprieties to sexual misconduct, the incidents have highlighted the importance of adhering to the legal requirements and ethical standards governing religious organizations.

Navigating legal requirements for religious organizations can be a complex and daunting task. While these organizations enjoy significant legal protections, they are also subject to various legal requirements that are specific to their religious context. For example, religious organizations are exempt from certain taxes, but they are also required to register with the government and provide financial disclosures. This requires a thorough understanding of the legal landscape and a commitment to compliance.

It is equally important to uphold ethical standards and maintain public trust in faith communities. These organizations have a vital role to play in fostering social cohesion, promoting moral values, and providing support to vulnerable populations. However, when their leaders engage in unethical behavior, the consequences can be devastating. Congregants and the public lose faith in the organization, and the organization's ability to fulfill its mission is compromised.

To promote ethical leadership and instill accountability, religious organizations must establish clear ethical codes and enforce them rigorously. This includes scrutinizing the behavior of leaders, reporting misconduct to authorities, and imposing appropriate sanctions when necessary. It also involves creating a culture of transparency and openness that encourages congregants to report any wrongdoing they witness.

Navigating legal requirements and upholding ethical standards are critical components of effective leadership in religious organizations. By doing so, these organizations can ensure that they fulfill their mission, maintain public trust, and foster a culture of integrity and accountability.

Conclusion

Thank you for taking this journey with me. The responsibility entrusted to you in safeguarding the sacred elements of your community of faith is indeed deserving of the time and commitment you've invested. Whether elected or appointed, you hold one of the most sacred responsibilities—to lead and serve your church in a manner that ensures its protection.

To fulfill this sacred duty, adopting a proactive and comprehensive approach to risk management is paramount. This involves paying close attention to four key areas: governance, protecting people, safeguarding property, and preserving reputation. Through the implementation of the strategies and best practices outlined in each of these sections, you can effectively mitigate the risks faced by your congregation, ensuring the safety and well-being of your members while safeguarding the reputation of your church community.

It is crucial for you to recognize that risk management is not an optional addition to your duties but an essential component. By prioritizing risk management, you will exemplify your dedication to serving your community of faith and preserving the sacred elements of your church. In doing so, you will undoubtedly provide peace of mind to members, employees, and volunteers, allowing them to focus on the spiritual growth and development at the core of your church community.

This book serves as a valuable tool for the church officers, also known as heroes, who are passionate about safeguarding the sacred elements of their communities of faith. Offering practical advice and guidance on identifying, assessing, and managing risks, *Protecting the Sacred: A Church Officer's Guide to Effective Risk Management* helps equip you to fulfill your duty of care and serve your congregation to the best of your ability. Through the adoption of a comprehensive approach to risk management, you can contribute to the long-term success and sustainability of your church community. May this knowledge empower you as you continue to lead and serve your community of faith with dedication and purpose.

APPENDIX 1

Sample Accident Investigation Form

Church Name:_____

Injured Party Name:_____

Employment Status:
Full-time ☐   Part-time ☐   Non-Employee ☐

☐ Near Miss
☐ First Aid Administered
☐ Medical Treatment Needed

Date of Incident: _____

Time of Injury: _____ ☐ AM ☐ PM

WITNESSES

Name: _____ Telephone: _____
Name: _____ Telephone: _____
Name: _____ Telephone: _____
Name: _____ Telephone: _____

CHAUNA-KAYE POTTINGER

Description of the Incident:
_____
_____
_____

Contributing Factors and Corrective Actions:
_____
_____
_____
_____
_____

APPENDIX 2

Church Security Officer Sample Job Description

The Church Safety Officer is a vital position appointed by the [insert selection body responsible for appointing church officers] of [insert church name] during the selection of church officers. A successful candidate should be highly organized, possess thorough knowledge of the local church organizational structure, and be familiar with the church members. Impeccable people skills, sound and mature judgment, and respect for strict confidential procedures associated with various aspects of accident review and investigation are essential.

As an esteemed member of the church board, the Church Safety Officer will also serve on the safety committee, tasked to support the Church Safety Officer, and assist in carrying out all aspects of the loss control program for all church activities.

Primary Objective:

The Church Safety Officer's top priority is the prevention of accidents. With the assistance of the safety committee, the Church Safety Officer can help the church achieve a position of taking corrective action consistently after each accident, thereby reducing major causes of losses at the church.

Requirements of the Role:

Regular Meetings:
The Church Safety Officer is expected to meet with the safety committee on a frequent basis and record minutes on at least a quarterly basis. If the church is too small to adequately form a safety committee, safety concerns can be addressed by the Church Safety Officer during monthly church staff/board meetings.

Controlling Accidents:
The primary method of controlling accidents will be a formal investigation and review of all accidents at the church, including both actual accidents and near-miss accidents. At each regularly scheduled meeting, the safety officer is responsible for providing the following information:

1. The injured person's activity at the time of the accident
2. How the injured person was injured
3. The unsafe act committed

Identification of Hazardous Conditions:
In addition to personal injury accident investigations, the Church Safety Officer should investigate property losses to determine such items as:

1. Description of the property
2. How the property was damaged
3. Any unsafe act that led to the property damage
4. Any hazardous conditions present
5. Where possible, supply a photograph of damaged property.

To determine the underlying causes of all accidents, the Church Safety Officer shall use the following procedures:

1. Visit the scene.
2. Interview witnesses to the accident.
3. Check for causes resulting from anyone's actions, dangerous practices, inability, disobeying rules, etc.
4. Check for poor housekeeping.
5. Determine if there was defective equipment.
6. Determine if there was improper apparel.
7. Record information of any other poor conditions.

Actions to Avoid:
The Church Safety Officer should avoid the following in carrying out their duties:

1. Attempting to pin the blame on an individual
2. Assuming there is just one cause for an accident

3. Assigning causes of accidents that are too general or vague
4. Determining causes of an accident without investigation
5. Attempting to take the place of the church board/administration in corrective action
6. Investigation of sexual misconduct incidents. These cases are to be immediately reported to Human Resources.

The Church Safety Officer should avoid the release of information to anyone other than a claims representative of [Insert Insurance Company] or [Insert Position of Designated Church Administrator].

Safety Officer Duties in Church Activities
The Church Safety Officer will work closely with other departments within the church in securing (where required) certificates of insurance for church activities. An inventory of all church-sponsored activities will be made and prohibited activities will be identified, which include but are not restricted to [insert restricted activities]

Record Keeping
The Church Safety Officer will also maintain inventory of activities that require an extra degree of supervision, planning, and procedural guidelines, such as day camps, field

trips, hiking trips, bonfires and campfire socials, hayrides, skating, water skiing, and health-screening fairs.

Work with the activity sponsor to collect signed:

1. Medical consent forms
2. Liability waivers (where applicable)
3. Written rules and formal procedures for activities

Areas Requiring Professional Expertise:
The Church Safety Officer should review the following areas and ensure periodic inspections and/or repair by licensed professionals:

1. Boilers and mechanical equipment
2. Construction activities
3. Roof
4. Electrical wiring and equipment
5. Fire extinguishers and alarm systems
6. Heating/air conditioning systems
7. Cooking equipment
8. Vehicles

APPENDIX 3

Sample [Insert Church Name] Child Protection Policy

Purpose

The purpose of the [Insert Church Name] Child Protection Policy is to ensure the safety and well-being of children and young people participating in church activities. This policy aims to create a safe and nurturing environment for children by providing clear guidelines and procedures for all paid staff and volunteers.

Scope

This policy applies to all paid staff and volunteers of [Insert Church Name] who interact with, supervise, or have control over children and youth during church activities.

Key Principles and Commitments

To fulfill our commitment of protecting children, [Insert Church Name] has implemented the following Child Protection and Youth Abuse Prevention Program. All paid staff and volunteers must understand and adhere to these guidelines to help prevent child abuse and neglect. The program consists of:

1. Providing a safe and secure environment for children, youth, adults, members, volunteers, visitors, and paid staff.
2. Assessing an individual's suitability to supervise, oversee, and/or exert control over the activities of children and youth.
3. Implementing a screening process for paid staff and volunteers.
4. Establishing a system to respond to alleged victims of abuse and their families, as well as the alleged perpetrator.
5. Reducing the possibility of false accusations of abuse made against volunteers and paid staff.

Recruitment Process
1. Background checks: All staff and volunteers who potentially have access to children must undergo a comprehensive background check, including criminal records, if required by governing law.
2. Child protection training: Staff and volunteers must complete mandatory child protection training before interacting with children and youth. Training must be updated periodically as determined by the organization.
3. Required certifications: Staff and volunteers working directly with children must possess necessary professional certifications, as required by governing laws and regulations.

Identifying and Reporting Child Abuse or Neglect
1. Staff and volunteers must follow legal requirements for reporting suspected incidents of child abuse or neglect.
2. Confidentiality of the reporting process must be maintained to protect both the child and the alleged perpetrator.
3. If a staff member or volunteer witnesses an incident of child abuse or neglect, they must immediately report it to their supervisor or designated person in charge.

Interaction Guidelines
1. Physical contact must be appropriate for the age of the child and not involve any inappropriate touching.
2. Staff and volunteers must treat all children and youth with respect and dignity, using appropriate language and tone of voice.
3. Staff and volunteers must not single out a specific child for preferential treatment or engage in favoritism.
4. Staff and volunteers must not allow children to engage in bullying, harassment, or discrimination of any kind, and should report any such behavior immediately.

Procedures for Handling Child Protection Cases
1. Upon receiving a report of potential child abuse or neglect, **[Insert Church Name]** will ensure the safety of the child and take appropriate action.

2. All incidents will be thoroughly investigated, ensuring confidentiality is maintained.
3. The organization will cooperate fully with external organizations, such as law enforcement or child protective services, in the investigation and resolution of cases.
4. **[Insert Church Name]** will maintain records of all incidents and outcomes, ensuring all relevant parties are informed of the situation and resolutions.

[Insert Church Name] is committed to providing a safe and nurturing environment for children and youth participating in church activities. By following the guidelines and procedures outlined in this policy, we strive to minimize risks and ensure the welfare of all children under our care.

APPENDIX 4

Sample Job Description of Church Safety Committee Member

Overview:

The Church Safety Committee plays a crucial role in ensuring the safety, security, and well-being of all members, visitors, and property within the church community. Committee members work collaboratively to identify potential risks and hazards, develop and implement safety protocols and procedures, and provide guidance and support in emergency situations. This position requires a commitment to promoting a culture of safety and preparedness within the church environment.

Responsibilities:

Risk Assessment: Conduct regular assessments of the church premises to identify potential safety hazards, security vulnerabilities, and emergency risks.

Policy Development: Collaborate with church leadership to develop comprehensive safety policies, procedures, and protocols to address identified risks and ensure compliance with relevant regulations and standards.

Emergency Planning: Develop and maintain emergency response plans for various scenarios, including fire, medical emergencies, severe weather, and active threats. Coordinate drills and training exercises to ensure preparedness and readiness.

Security Measures: Evaluate and recommend security measures and technologies to enhance the physical security of the church property, including surveillance systems, access control measures, and perimeter security.

Training and Education: Provide training and education to church staff, volunteers, and congregation members on safety best practices, emergency response procedures, and crisis management strategies.

Incident Response: Serve as a resource and support during emergency situations, providing guidance and assistance to church personnel and congregants as needed. Coordinate communication and response efforts with external emergency services and authorities.

Community Outreach: Foster positive relationships with local law enforcement, emergency services, and community organizations to promote collaboration and mutual support in ensuring the safety and security of the church and surrounding community.

Documentation and Reporting: Maintain accurate records of safety inspections, incidents, and training activities. Prepare reports and recommendations for church leadership regarding safety-related matters.

Continual Improvement: Monitor and evaluate the effectiveness of safety initiatives and programs, soliciting feedback from stakeholders and implementing enhancements as needed to continually improve the church's safety and security posture.

Committee Participation: Attend regular safety committee meetings, actively contribute ideas and insights, and collaborate with fellow committee members to fulfill the committee's mission and objectives.

Qualifications:
- Commitment to the mission and values of the church community.
- Strong interpersonal and communication skills, with the ability to work effectively with diverse groups of people.
- Knowledge of safety and security principles, practices, and regulations.
- Experience in emergency planning, response, or related fields preferred.
- Ability to maintain confidentiality and handle sensitive information with discretion.
- Strong organizational and problem-solving skills, with attention to detail.
- Availability to participate in meetings, training sessions, and emergency response activities as needed.

Note: This job description is intended to outline the general responsibilities and qualifications for the Church Safety Committee Member role and may be adapted to reflect the specific needs and requirements of individual church

APPENDIX 5

Cyber Risk Vulnerability Checklist

Network Security:	
Are firewalls installed and properly configured to filter incoming and outgoing traffic?	☐
Is the church's Wi-Fi network secured with encryption and a strong password?	☐
Are regular vulnerability scans and penetration tests conducted to identify weaknesses in the network?	☐
Endpoint Security:	
Are all computers, laptops, and mobile devices used within the church equipped with up-to-date antivirus and antimalware software?	☐
Are operating systems and software applications regularly updated with security patches and fixes?	☐
Are strong password policies enforced for accessing devices and accounts?	☐
Data Protection:	
Is sensitive data, such as financial records, donor information, and personal data, encrypted both in transit and at rest?	☐
Are regular backups of critical data performed, and are they stored securely offsite or in the cloud?	☐
Are access controls implemented to restrict unauthorized access to sensitive information?	☐

Email Security:	
Are email filtering and spam detection mechanisms in place to prevent phishing attacks and malware distribution?	☐
Are employees and volunteers trained to recognize suspicious emails and avoid clicking on malicious links or attachments?	☐
Is multi-factor authentication enabled for email accounts to enhance security?	☐
Website Security:	
Is the church's website hosted on a secure and reputable platform?	☐
Are web applications regularly scanned for vulnerabilities, such as SQL injection and cross-site scripting (XSS)?	☐
Are SSL/TLS certificates used to encrypt data transmitted between the website and visitors' browsers?	☐
User Awareness and Training:	
Are employees, volunteers, and staff members trained on cybersecurity best practices and procedures?	☐
Are they educated about the risks of social engineering tactics, such as phishing, pretexting, and tailgating?	☐
Are regular security awareness campaigns conducted to reinforce good cybersecurity habits?	☐
Incident Response Preparedness:	
Does the church have an incident response plan in place to guide actions in the event of a cyber-attack?	☐
Are roles and responsibilities clearly defined, and is there a designated incident response team?	☐
Is there a communication plan for notifying stakeholders, including congregation members, in the event of a data breach or security incident?	☐

Physical Security:	
Are servers, networking equipment, and other IT infrastructure components housed in a secure, access-controlled location?	☐
Are visitor access policies enforced to prevent unauthorized individuals from gaining physical access to sensitive areas?	☐
Is surveillance and monitoring conducted to detect and deter unauthorized activities?	☐
Vendor and Third-Party Risk Management:	
Does the church assess the cybersecurity practices and controls of third-party vendors and service providers?	☐
Are contracts and agreements with vendors reviewed to ensure they include provisions for cybersecurity responsibilities and liabilities?	☐
Is there a process for monitoring and auditing third-party compliance with security requirements?	☐
Regulatory Compliance:	
Are policies and procedures in place to address compliance requirements specific to the church's jurisdiction and industry sector?	☐
Are regular audits conducted to assess compliance with regulatory standards and guidelines?	☐

Notes

Chapter 1
1. Moses v. the Diocese of Colorado, 863 P.2d 310 (Colo. 1993).

Chapter 2
1. Michael Elliot, *Risk Management Principles and Practices* (Malvern, PA: The Institutes, 2018).

Chapter 7
1. John Maxwell, *Life Wisdom: Quotes from John Maxwell: Insights on Leadership* (Nashville, TN: Broadman & Holman), P. 153

Chapter 8
1. Gregory Love, Kimberlee Norris, Georgia McKnight, *Sexual Abuse Awareness Training* (Fort Worth, TX: Ministry Safe, 2022).

Chapter 9.
1. Panchuk, Michelle. 2018. "The Shattered Spiritual Self: Philosophical Exploration of Religious Trauma." *Res Philosophica*. 95 (3): 505–530.

Chapter 10
1. American Academy of Pediatrics, American Public Health Association, & National Resource Center for Health and Safety in Child Care and Early Education. (2019). *Caring for our children: National health and safety performance standards: Guidelines for early care and education programs (4th ed.)*.
2. "Supervision Ratios and Group Sizes." Childcare.gov. https://childcare.gov/consumer-education/ratios-and-group-sizes

Chapter 14
1. "Motor Vehicle," National Safety Council, 2024, https://injuryfacts.nsc.org/motor-vehicle/overview/introduction/.
2. "10 Essentials of Transportation Safety," Church Mutual Insurance, 2022, https://www.churchmutual.com/98/Safety-Resources.

Chapter 16
1. Richard Hammer, "Ministerial Exception," Church Law & Tax, 2020, https://www.churchlawandtax.com/stay-legal/clergy-law/ministerial-exception/.

Chapter 22
1. "Billion-Dollar Weather and Climate Disasters," NOAA National Centers for Environmental Information, 2024, https://www.ncei.noaa.gov/access/billions/.

Milton Keynes UK
Ingram Content Group UK Ltd.
UKHW050718010724
444982UK00014B/941

9 798893 332759